MARTYRS
AND
MIRACLES

BY CAROLYN TRICKEY-BAPTY

TESTAMENT
BOOKS

This 2001 edition is published by Testament Books™,
an imprint of Random House Value Publishing, Inc.
280 Park Avenue, New York, NY 10017
by arrangement with Ottenheimer Publishers, Inc.
5 Park Center Court, Suite 300, Owings Mills, MD 21117.

Testament Books™ and design are trademarks of
Random House Value Publishing, Inc.

Random House
New York • Toronto • London • Sydney • Auckland
http://www.randomhouse.com/

Printed and bound in the United States of America.

A catalog record for this title is available from the Library of Congress.

ISBN: 0-517-16403-5

9 8 7 6 5 4 3 2 1

CONTENTS

A WORD OF THANKS

It would have been impossible to write this book without the generous help and support from lots of friends and my family. Thanking them all just doesn't seem like enough, but here goes:

Thanks to Bill Beeton, who so kindly downloaded information about saints from his PC; to the library staff at McMaster University, who helped me find what I needed and allowed me to take it home; to Bill Calvert who found me the music for "When the saints go marching in"; and to my dear friends Chandrani and Mahendra Wijayasinghe, who sent me lots of interesting material on Buddhism.

The people who helped with the children's chapter are many, and the section would simply not exist without them. Many thanks to Pearl, Phyllis and the children from Bellefair United Church; to Kevin Campbell, Elizabeth Vasas and the children from Our Lady of Peace School; and the children from Holy Trinity School. The organization and hard work by Kathleen Fitzpatrick made my interviews at the schools a piece of cake and I'd like to say a special thank you, Kathleen! Many thanks to Barbara Maguire who put me in touch with all the right people. And what can I say about Laurie Chisholm—my good friend who is always there for me—once again helped out by organizing the Sunday School children.

To the children who were interviewed, thank you for your thought-provoking questions and fascinating insights on saints. I enjoyed talking with each one of you and I hope I was able to answer your questions satisfactorily. And to the parents, I appreciate you allowing your children to participate in the project—with a special word of thanks going to Joanne, Pam, and Steve and Bev.

Many others played a different role, but all contributed to me 'getting it done.' I'd like to mention Drs. Robert Pearman and James Spring, who helped get me back on my feet again after Jerred's birth. And a very special thank you to my friend and midwife, Mina Niak. Your phone calls, visits and words of concern and encouragement meant more to me than you could ever know. To my editor, Julie Williams, thanks once again for your hard work and help via the telephone!

To my dear friends: Claire Gerus, thank you for guiding my life in this new direction; Allan and Susan Lappin and Ryan Jenkins, whose love and support I can always rely on; Ann Silverman, whose insight is always inspiring; Amy Gerlock, your words of wisdom I'll always remember; Carol Jones, thanks for listening! Without all of your encouragement, I don't know if I could have kept going.

And finally, and most importantly, to my family: Stella, thank you so much for your encouragement and loving support; Simon and Silvana, your caring, understanding and love means so much to all of us; and Al and Lisa, your help was crucial not only for me, but for Eric as well. Love ya' lots! What can I say to Mom and Dad? Without you, the book could have never been written. Hugs and kisses from both me and Jerred!

And to my loving husband, Eric. We'll always be there for each other. I love you.

Lots of love and thanks to all of you!

PREFACE

Growing up in the province of Québec, Canada, I was literally surrounded by saints, from Saint Anne to Saint Zotique. I attended Saint Paul's Anglican Church in Lachine, drove to meet with friends in Saint Anne de Bellevue, visited the sanctuary at Saint Anne de Beaupré, took guests to Saint Joseph's Oratory and Notre Dame de Grâce (Our Lady of Grace) Cathedral in Montréal, sat by the water's edge on the Saint Lawrence River, walked along Saint Catherine's Street in downtown Montréal, took drives to Saint Thérèse-en-Hâute—well, you get my drift. But I never once thought about the origin of these names, until I was approached to research *Martyrs and Miracles: The Inspiring Lives of Saints and Martyrs*. Suddenly, I had lots of questions! I immersed myself in saints—at least as much as my four-month-old son would allow—and became totally fascinated.

How many saints were there? Well, there literally seemed to be thousands! And was Saint Anne de Bellevue the same Anne as Saint Anne de Beaupré? I had simply thought that saints were connected to the Roman Catholic Church, but was that so? How could it be if I had attended Saint Paul's Anglican Church? The more I looked around me, the more saints I found. Hospitals named Saint Peter's or Saint Joseph's. Cities like Saint Louis, San Diego and San Francisco. Vacation spots called Saint Kitts, Saint Lucia and

Saint Petersburg. Why, there's even a football team called the "Saints"!

The more I looked, the more I began to realize that saints do not "belong" to the Roman Catholics. Indeed, they are not specific to Christianity. And I was fascinated by the history, so meticulously documented, about all saints, how it had started and what happens today. I looked at saints in other religions and saw what an impact they had on the everyday person. I began to realize how much of the history and culture of Western Civilization is richly interwoven with the history of Christianity and the tremendous popularity of Christian saints. The tapestry of our world today contains the colorful threads of the heroic and virtuous lives of the saints.

Each one of us needs a hero. As children we may look to sports stars or perhaps family members. Later, it may be a boss, a politician, a friend, maybe even a movie or pop star. But, sooner or later, we come to realize the human foibles of our hero. And we are disappointed, disenchanted. The saints do not betray us. Their lives are shining examples of love, kindness, patience, and virtue. They are heroes through time.

Although this book was researched with much care, it is not intended to be a scholarly work of reference. With many different stories and legends of the same saint, it is sometimes difficult to sort out fact from fiction. Any discrepancies you may find are likely to be my interpretations. Please use the Bibliography at the end for further reading and study. There are several dictionaries of saints, including *Butler's Lives of the Saints*, the Oxford and Penguin dictionaries, all of which are interesting to peruse. As Cardinal Newman wrote:

And this is all that is known, and more than all—yet nothing to what the angels know—of the life of a servant of God, who sinned and repented and did penance and washed out his sins, and became a Saint, and reigns with Christ in heaven.

—*Carolyn Trickey-Bapty*

WHO BELIEVES IN SAINTS?

Almighty and everlasting God, in whom we live and move and have our being, who hast created us for Thyself, so that we can find rest only in Thee; grant unto us purity of heart and strength of purpose, that no selfish passion may hinder us from knowing Thy will, no weakness from doing it; but in Thy light may we see light clearly, and in Thy service find perfect freedom; through Jesus Christ our Lord. AMEN.

—Saint Augustine
(4th century)

When you hear the word *saint*, do you automatically think, "Roman Catholic"? Or perhaps you remember that the early Apostles (Saint Paul, Saint Luke, etc.) are called saints. Or that the church you attend is called Saint Joseph's. Where did all these saints come from, anyway? And how do they relate to us in everyday life?

Even though the majority of us associate saints with Christianity, and more specifically with the Roman Catholic Church, saints have also been honored in other major religions. Judaism, Islam, Hinduism, Buddhism, and Confucianism, for example, consider holy people who have lived exemplary lives to be equal to those figures Christians know as saints.

For some, the idea that one believes in saints, or in a saint, implies some sort of idol worship. Indeed this was, and is, the major criticism of the veneration of saints—and the reason why Martin Luther, John Calvin, and other Protestants established their independent churches. However, when we examine the early Christian church, we soon discover that the faithful followers of Christ were first called saints by the Apostle Paul. By choice, they had set themselves apart from the traditional religious beliefs of their day—to the point of persecution, torture, and death—trying to live according to the example set forth by Christ.

Gradually the concept of sainthood became interwoven with the notion of martyrs and heroes, charismatic figures who were looked up to as examples of how to live a good, kindhearted life. Miracles were attributed to them before and after their deaths. Their love for their fellow man transcended death, and those left behind knew that their beloved saint was still with them, even in death.

It is not hard to understand, then, why every major religion has a concept of sainthood. For in all religions, there have been leaders who have died for their beliefs, whose love for their fellow human beings has endeared them to mankind. Most of what we know about saints, however, comes from early Christian and Roman Catholic tradition.

It is these saints, their lives and legends, that this book largely discusses, while briefly touching on holy men and women from other religions.

Who believes in saints? People from all walks of life, old and young, from every culture—saints belong to us all.

CHAPTER ONE

WHAT IS A SAINT?

O most merciful Redeemer, Friend, and Brother,
May we know Thee more clearly,
Love Thee more dearly,
Follow Thee more nearly;
For ever and ever. AMEN.

—Saint Richard Chichester
(13th century)

When you think of a saint, what comes to mind? Is it Great Aunt Martha, who is "a saint" for putting up with you all these years? Or perhaps it's the saint for whom your church is named? Or maybe it's your patron saint, the saint who has special meaning for you?

The word *saint* comes from the Latin word *sanctus*, meaning holy or consecrated. The Greeks and Romans used the word *sanctus* to describe various persons—emperors, gods, even deceased relatives. Through the centuries, the word evolved to denote a holy person who is charitable, patient, and mild-mannered. And in the early Christian church, according to a letter from Paul to the Romans (Rom. 1:7), anyone who declared himself to be a follower of Christ was called a saint: "To all God's beloved in Rome, who are called to be saints: Grace to you and peace from God our Father and the Lord Jesus Christ."

In his letter to the Romans, Paul also mentioned that there were saints in Jerusalem who needed help. Would the churches put a little bit aside each week? For Paul, the faithful followers of Christ were saints, and he drew on his background in the Jewish faith to explain how they had become sanctified. In the Old Testament, the word *holy* described something or someone that was meant to be set apart by God. There are holy days, holy places of worship, and a holy people—the Israelites, who were chosen by God. God gave the Hebrews the Law by which to live, which was basically the Ten Commandments and a long set of rules. Paul realized that the Law in itself could not make people holy. Rather, to follow the example of The Holy One, Jesus Christ, they had to state their wish to become holy. Thus, the ceremony of baptism by water symbolized washing away the old self and sanctifying the new, holy self. According to Paul in his letter to the Corinthians (1 Cor. 6:11), Christians had become the new holy people, set apart by God: "But you were washed, you were sanctified, you were justified in the name of the Lord Jesus Christ and in the Spirit of our God."

In today's usage, however, the word *saint* usually describes a person who leads an unusually virtuous life as compared to most others—just as Paul wrote to his saints, "Follow my example, as I follow the example of Christ," in 1 Cor. 10:33.

WHAT DO ALL SAINTS HAVE IN COMMON?

All saints have the following in common:

* They lead remarkable lives of heroic virtue.
* They link the known with the unknown by serving as communicators between the faithful and their God.
* They are deemed holy men and women, through whom God works to effect changes in people's lives.

WHY DO PEOPLE BELIEVE IN SAINTS?

Many people believe that saints help them in their everyday lives, that they can be called upon in times of need, and that they perform miraculous cures. The early Christians were very familiar with their saints, who were often members of their families or their local church. How many of us have felt a special closeness to a relative or friend who has passed on? For example, although my grandfather died over thirty years ago, I still feel his presence on occasion. And I'll ask him to watch over my son, or my husband on his way to work. My grandfather is not a saint, but he certainly was a good man.

Today, people who believe in saints also feel a close, personal connection to them. They are aware of the exemplary lives the saints led, and they choose to model their own lives after them. And sometimes miracles do occur. Faith can transcend all.

HOW DO SAINTS HELP US?

Saints help us in various ways. Through their unconditional love for others, they show us how to lead good, kind, charitable lives. We don't have to give up everything we own, or join a monastery or convent, but we can learn how to treat others better. And this more often than not results in people being kind and loving toward us as well.

Saints also help us by way of prayer. We can pray to the saints, asking for specific needs or simply telling of our daily activities. They provide us with their guidance, friendship, and love from heaven. And, sometimes, when our need is great and our faith is pure, our prayers to them result in astounding miracles!

HOW CLOSE ARE SAINTS TO GOD?

Saints are men and women like ourselves, but they chose to dedicate their lives to God, following the example Jesus set. Because each one is an individual, every sainthood is unique as well. Some led lives of complete poverty, some were literally "soldiers of God," some spent their time in prayer and meditation, some were missionaries, some studied and interpreted holy writings. We can say, then, that they lived lives quite apart from the ordinary concerns of most human beings. While saints cannot be classified in the realm of angels, they may abide in the same heaven. But because saints were human, people feel akin to the saints and pray to them because of their closeness to God.

CAN SAINTS COMMUNICATE WITH US?

Many people believe that saints communicate with them on a daily basis. And they talk to the saints as well. Saints can communicate by giving us visions or through "interior speech," when they silently speak to us through our minds. Teresa of Avila, who later became a saint herself, experienced such communication. While a young nun at a convent, she began to neglect her prayers and as a result felt unworthy to follow God. One day, while she was praying before a picture of Jesus, she "felt Saint Mary Magdalene come to [her] assistance."[1] From that day on, she found the courage to devote herself more fully to God. She withdrew more and more from social activities and spent more of her time in prayer. On one occasion, she asked God what she could do that would be most pleasing to Him, and she heard His answer within her soul, "I will not have you hold conversation with men, but with angels."[2]

Anne Gordon's *A Book of Saints* details the story of a saint's communication with John Ounan, a court stenographer. According to Gordon, a prominent man had been arrested for molestation. But because he was so well known, the case was dismissed. However, once the district attorney found out about the deal, he had the man rearrested. As the court recorder, John was told to cover up the judge's initial wrongdoing. Either he compromised his ethics or he would lose his job. He decided to ask Saint Thomas More, patron saint of lawyers, for guidance. As he prayed, he felt the saint's presence and knew that he had to do what was right. Although he was fired from his job two days later, John has always strived to follow the truth ever since.[3]

CAN SAINTS APPEAR BEFORE US?

Saints have appeared to men and women throughout the ages. Legends tell of Joan of Arc hearing the voices of Saint Catherine of Alexandria, Saint Margaret of Antioch, and the archangel Saint Michael, who told her that she was destined to save France from the English.

Mary, the mother of Jesus, is said to have appeared to humankind most often. Most notably, Mary appeared to Saint Bernard and later to Saint Bernadette (of Lourdes fame).

According to legend, the Virgin Mary appeared to Saint Bernard during a prolonged period of anguish when he was unable to write anything, moistening his lips with her breast milk to make his words more inspirational. Shrines have now been built honoring her famous visits in Mexico and Portugal.

As long as we remain open to the possibility of saints appearing before us, we never know what might happen!

ARE SAINTS GHOSTS OR SPIRITS?

We usually think of a ghost as being a pale, shadowy figure resembling someone who has died. Because saints often appear after their deaths, we may misinterpret them as ghosts or spirits. Ghosts are thought to be the souls of human beings who have died and have chosen to remain close to the earthly plane. Some ghosts wish to comfort or protect those left behind. Others suffered a death so traumatic, they have trouble accepting that they are no longer alive.

But saints are not ghosts or spirits. Their souls have ascended into heaven, and it is from heaven that we ask them to intercede for us.

BESIDES THE ROMAN CATHOLIC CHURCH, DO OTHER CHRISTIAN CHURCHES HAVE SAINTS?

Saints have never been honored, or venerated, in other Christian denominations to the extent that they are in Roman Catholicism. Many Protestants know little about saints and have shunned them since the Reformation, believing that veneration is a type of idol worship.

The Church of England has added a few saints to its calendar. Perhaps the most notable is Saint Charles, who was crowned Charles I, king of England, in 1625. He was executed on January 30, 1649 for his defense of the Anglican Church and resistance to Parliament. His body secretly buried in Windsor Castle, he became a widely acclaimed martyr. Today, services are held at the Church of Saint Martin-in-the-Fields and in London's Trafalgar Square on his feast day. Since 1928, the Church of England has set aside November 8—one week after All Saints' Day—as "Saints, Doctors, Missionaries, and Martyrs Day" to commemorate the "unnamed saints of the nation."

Although the articles of religion for the Anglican Church in Canada state that "invocation of Saints, is a fond thing vainly invented, and grounded upon no warranty of Scripture, but rather repugnant to the Word of God,"[4] saints are increasingly popular among Anglicans today. A new liturgical book published by the Anglican Church in Canada contains prayers for the saints on their feast days in its calendar. The English Reformers' original problem with saints was that custom decreed the only way to pray to God was through the saints. The Anglican Church now has allowed for the invocation of saints within its liturgy—the prayers, acts, and ceremonies used in public worship.

More recently, the Episcopal Church has nominated four women to be added to their liturgical Calendar of Saints in 1997. These are Elizabeth Cady Stanton, Amelia Bloomer, Sojourner Truth, and Harriet Tubman, all pioneers in the antislavery and women's rights movements. Harriet Tubman, a former slave, was not an Episcopalian, but was honored on February 19, 1995, as a saint in the church where her owner had been baptized. After fleeing to Pennsylvania and freedom in 1849, Harriet returned to Maryland fifteen times to help other slaves escape, believing that she was being directed by God. She died in Auburn, New York, in 1913.

In Eastern Orthodoxy, saints have also had a central place. Together with the Moscovite patriarch, the Russian Orthodox Church obtained supreme authority to canonize saints. And many Orthodox churches are adorned with the icons, or ornate pictures, of saints. The cult of the individual saint never developed in Eastern Orthodoxy to the extent that it did in the West, but was replaced by a tendency to venerate saints in general.

ARE SAINTS REFERRED TO BY ANY OTHER TITLES?
Apostles and martyrs were first referred to as saints during the fifth century. But before that, they were addressed much more casually. One can find scratched on the walls of catacombs: "Paul and Peter, pray for me." However, the word "holy" was a term of respect for someone whose office had a religious nature. One might write to the emperor of Rome as "Sancte imperator," or "Holy Emperor." One referred to a deceased bishop as "Bishop Gregory of holy memory" but his living counterpart as "Your Holiness." Until lately, bishops in France were referred to as "Grandeur"; archbishops in England are still called "Grace"; but only the pope remains "His Holiness."

CHAPTER TWO

HOW DOES ONE BECOME A SAINT?

Give me, O lord, a steadfast heart,
which no unworthy affection may drag downwards;
give me an unconquered heart,
which no tribulation can wear out;
give me an upright heart,
which no unworthy purpose may tempt aside.
Bestow on me also, O Lord my God,
understanding to know you,
diligence to seek you,
wisdom to find you,
and a faithfulness that may finally embrace you,
through Jesus Christ our Lord. AMEN.

—Saint Thomas Aquinas
(13th century)

As defined in the Webster's New World Dictionary, a saint is a holy person, one who is very meek and charitable. This definition can thus apply to holy persons of any religion. However, the word *saint* has become identified more with Christianity, and especially with the Roman Catholic Church, which has laid down very specific rules as to the eligibility of a person to be a saint. This chapter looks at the Christian concept of sainthood as seen through the eyes of Roman Catholicism.

In the early days, to become a saint it was simply enough to die professing faith in Christ. The saint's bodily remains were removed and entombed, and the date and place entered on the official record of the Church. But sometimes this was not as easy as it sounds. What about the heretics or schismatics (people who broke away to form a different sect) who were put to death professing the name of Christ? How could they be saints if they were not members of the Church? In cases such as these, the qualification of sainthood became subject to the local bishop's approval.

It was not until A.D. 993 that the first formal request for sainthood was made to the Vatican in Rome, recommending that the bishop Ulric be considered a saint on the basis of his holy life and the miracles he performed.

Gradually, Rome's sanction increased the dignity and importance of the veneration of saints, until Pope Alexander III finally decreed in the twelfth century that all cases of canonization were to be reviewed by the Roman Catholic Church. From then until the seventeenth century, the process became more explicit. In 1634, Pope Urban VIII decreed the broad outlines of rules for the approval of *cultus*, or the veneration of a saint by public acts. This laid the foundation for the distinction between a "blessed" and a "saint." All the thousands of previous canonizations were not called into question, but a spontaneous public veneration of a person was no longer regarded as the first step toward canonization.

At the same time, the Roman Church forbade any images depicting the person with a halo until Rome declared him blessed. The process has now become so rigorous that in 1977 there were only 177 *officially* canonized saints.

WHAT ARE THE STEPS TO SAINTHOOD?

The basic steps to sainthood are:

* nomination,
* beatification, and
* canonization.

HOW DOES ONE GET NOMINATED TO BE A SAINT?

To nominate a person for sainthood, people from the local church where the proposed saint lived or performed work gather writings by the person or about the person's life and present them to the local bishop. While the bishop is responsible for verifying the saintliness of the person, it is often the local church people and their priest who press for the case to continue. They devote years to raise funds and keep the name of the saint-to-be in the spotlight. It is their hard work and dedication to the cause that ultimately propels the name of a saint to be brought before the pope.

WHAT IS BEATIFICATION?

Beatification is the next step toward sainthood. The Church authorizes public veneration on a local level, with a mass and an Office of Prayer in the name of the person honored. The servant of God is declared *beatus*, or blessed, which up until the early 1600s meant the same as *sanctus*, or saint. The Church can revoke this designation for any good reason, and does not require worldwide veneration. Nonetheless the Church does begin a process of extensive inquiries into the life and into writings of and about the person.

For an individual to be declared blessed, the congregation must determine that the person led an exceptionally heroic, virtuous life, or that the person was martyred.

First, the local bishop or committee collects all the writings, talks to witnesses, and ensures that there has been no public veneration of the person. Documents verifying this information are then sent to Rome, where they are examined by a group of cardinals, a section of the Congregation of Rites, called the Sacred Congregation for the Causes of the Saints. If the cardinals' opinion is favorable, the pope declares the cause for sainthood to begin.

Church officials then make further inquiries into the life and relics of the person at his or her local church. Then, judgment is made in Rome on the heroism of the person's virtue or the reality of the martyrdom. If either is proved, the pope declares that this person may be called venerable.

If a person was martyred, miracles need not be proven, and official veneration results. If the person did not die as a martyr, then two or more miracles after death must be proven, with the help of a physician or another expert. Once experts offer acceptable proof, the pope declares that beatification may proceed, and the saint is venerated, or called blessed, by the local church. The pope can then go further and canonize the blessed.

WHAT IS CANONIZATION?

The word *canon*, or *canonization*, comes from the Greek word *kanōn*, meaning measuring rod or rule. Canonization is an act defined by a set of rules used to measure a person's holiness. In its most literal sense, a canon is a list of saints; therefore, to add a name to that list is called canonization.

In order to be canonized, the blessed's or beatus's life is again examined, but this time the emphasis is on proof that the blessed has performed two or more miracles since beatification. This is to ensure that God continues to work through the blessed. Much time often elapses during this period. Although originally set down by Canon Law, recently this requirement has often been dispensed with. In 1935, Saint John Fisher and Saint Thomas More were canonized without proof that they had performed miracles.

Once all the requirements have been met, the pope pronounces the final judgment in a special rite that is held in Saint Peter's Basilica:

> To the honor of the holy and undivided Trinity . . .
> We decree and define that the blessed [name] is a saint,
> and We enter his name in the roll of saints, ordering
> that his memory be religiously venerated every year by
> the Church throughout the world. . . ."[5]

The person is now canonized and is referred to by the title of saint before his first name. Public veneration is now permitted on a worldwide level, and the saint's feast day is added to the Roman Martyrology.

WHO IS THE DEVIL'S ADVOCATE?

The Devil's Advocate is the common name for the Promoter of the Faith, a cardinal of the Congregation of Rites, whose job is to meticulously examine the life of a proposed saint. He looks at all the evidence of miracles and details of the life and questions or objects to any aspects he feels may make the person unworthy of sainthood. The Devil's Advocate had so many questions about Elizabeth Seton—such as "Did she attempt suicide or only contemplate it?" and "What was the nature of her relationship with a close family friend?"— that it took twenty years before they were all satisfactorily answered!

HOW LONG DOES IT TAKE TO BECOME A SAINT?

After the cause has been introduced fifty years must pass before the final virtues are examined and the person is declared venerable. And at that point, if the person is not a martyr, two miracles must be proven before the saint is classified as blessed and venerated locally. The case must be reexamined and more miracles proved before canonization is realized. It can take centuries before everything is in order. It took Saint Catherine of Siena 81 years to be canonized; Saint Joan of Arc, 464 years; and Saint John of the Cross, 135 years. But it took Saint Bernadette of Lourdes only 54 years to be declared a saint.

CAN POPES BECOME SAINTS?

Not only can popes become saints, but seventy-seven of them already have been given the title—the latest being Saint Pius X, who died on August 20, 1914, and was canonized in 1954. Most of the popes elevated to sainthood were leaders of the early Church and were martyred as a result of their position. In fact, every pope, except two, from Saint Peter, who died in A.D. 67, to Saint Symmachus, who died in A.D. 514, is a saint.

CAN A SAINT BE "DECANONIZED"?

Very few saints have been stripped of the title of sanctus, or decanonized, but many saints have been reduced to local veneration. The reform of the Roman calendar in 1969 standardized saints' feast days by selecting a group of saints from all ages, backgrounds, and countries to be venerated by the Church worldwide. At the same time, some of the saints were taken out entirely due to the lack of historical evidence of their existence. The popular Saint Catherine of Alexandria was removed from the calendar, and Saint Christopher, Saint George, and Saint Vitus were reduced to local veneration, meaning they are only officially venerated by those churches that house their relics. Saint Wilgefortis, the patron of unhappy marriages, had his cult suppressed in 1969. So did Saint Eustace, who was invoked by people in difficult situations (he was roasted to death), and Saint Barbara, whose patronage included miners and gunners.

ARE THE STEPS TOWARD SAINTHOOD STILL FOLLOWED TODAY?

The easiest way to answer this question is to trace the steps recently followed by the Roman Catholic Church in the case of two North Americans: one who is beatified, Blessed

Brother André, and one who is canonized, Saint Elizabeth Ann Seton. As you will see, the process is a very lengthy one, requiring much patience on the side of the petitioners and much investigation on the side of the Church.

BLESSED BROTHER ANDRÉ

Better known as the Miracle Man of Montréal, Brother André was born Alfred Bessette on August 9, 1845, in the small village of Saint Gregoire d'Iberville, just south of Montréal in Canada. He was a very pious youth. At the age of eighteen, his parents died and Alfred roamed North America, working wherever he could. Finally, he returned to Québec and, in 1870, entered the Congregation of Holy Cross as a working brother, taking the name André. (Upon taking holy orders, people often take the name of a saint or holy person after whom they wish to model their lives.)

Brother André was deeply devoted to Saint Joseph, using Saint Joseph's oil whenever he was sick and rubbing a Saint Joseph's medal wrapped with cloth on his body. Eventually, he used this curative on others who were sick, often with amazing results. People with incurable diseases began to frequent the College of Notre Dame, and more miracles were documented. Finally, when Brother André was sixty-four years old, he was made the guardian of Saint Joseph's Oratory in Montréal, and the following year, in 1910, his healing miracles made headline news. Thousands of people from all over North America began to make pilgrimages to the site where this holy man lived. And thousands believed they had received cures.

On January 6, 1937, Brother André died. When he was buried a week later, his body showed no signs of decomposition. In fact, there were many reports of cures from people who had touched his body while it lay in state. The process to beatify him began almost immediately.

First, a biography of Brother André's life was written. Then a tribunal in Montréal conducted three trials to determine whether he had practiced—to a heroic degree—the virtues considered necessary for beatification. The Trial of Writings examined Brother André's very brief literary collection: three letters dictated to his family. The Information Trial interviewed dozens of people who witnessed André's virtues, and the Non-Cult Trial ensured that people were not anticipating his possible sainthood by offering public devotions.

In 1955, the results of these investigations were submitted to the Sacred Congregation of Rites, which took up the case in 1958. After three years of study, the cardinals recommended to the Pope that Brother André's cause be approved for further consideration. With Pope John XXIII's blessing, a new series of Apostolic Trials began, in which a representative from the Vatican reviewed the same material investigated by the Montréal Tribunals. And, as required by Canon Law, Brother André's tomb was opened in 1963, and his remains were identified. The investigators also inspected the heart of Brother André, which had been on display in a glass case in the Oratory Museum.

Over the next year a record of all the proceedings was prepared and submitted to the Congregation of Rites, which gave copies of it to nine judges, each of whom studied it for nine months and prepared a brief. On December 20, 1977, the briefs were turned over by the Congregation of Rites to the Congregation for the Causes of Saints. All the judges had reached a positive decision.

In the meantime, the bishops of Canada had requested that Pope Paul VI grant the cause of Brother André a dispensation from the law stating that fifty years must lapse between the death of a "servant of God" and the start of the final study of virtues. On June 11, 1977, the pope granted their request. On February 21, 1978, the Congregation for the Causes of Saints voted to ratify the judges' decision. In turn, on April 13, Pope Paul voted to ratify their decision, declaring Brother André "venerable."

In order for Brother André to be declared blessed, miracles must have occurred after his death. By the mid-1960s, the Congregation of Rites had over two dossiers of miracles from which to investigate. They chose to send the story of Joseph Audino's miraculous cure to the Congregation for the Causes of Saints in 1979:

> On July 24, 1958, while in his late forties, Joseph Audino was told he had reticulum cell sarcoma (a type of cancer that manifests in multiple organs and is thus very difficult to treat) and that he didn't have long to live. Although Joseph was not much of a church-going man, he had heard of Brother André. Joseph prayed to Brother André that night, asking him to tell his doctors what to do to save him. The next day the doctor tried an experimental treatment—he injected radioactive gold into Joseph's veins. The doctor thought it would shrink his swollen liver and relieve some of the pain.
>
> Three weeks later, there was no improvement. On August 14, Joseph was running a temperature of 105°, and his doctors believed he would die that night. Suddenly, Joseph went into a deep sleep, and when he woke up the next morning, he declared that he was cured! The doctors performed extensive tests but could find no evidence of cancer. (The staff at Saint Joseph's Oratory believe that Joseph Audino lived until 1982.)[6]

This miracle was backed by a 585-page medical report and more than 140 X rays. Members of the Congregations held sessions to hear witnesses and hired a team of medical specialists to verify Audino's cure. Finally, on May 23, 1982, Pope John Paul II formally declared the "Miracle Man of Montréal" Blessed Brother André Bessette.

SAINT ELIZABETH ANN SETON

Mother Seton is the first person born in the United States to be canonized by the Roman Catholic Church. She was born Elizabeth Ann Bayley on August 28, 1774, the second of three daughters, to Dr. Richard Bayley and his first wife, Catherine, in New York City. Her maternal grandfather was the Reverend Richard Charlton, the rector of Saint Andrew's Anglican Church on Staten Island, and Elizabeth was raised as an Episcopalian. At the age of nineteen, she married William Magee Seton.

Elizabeth's married life was a happy one, resulting in five children. William's business prospered for the first four years, allowing Elizabeth to participate in the social life of New York. Among other things, she was instrumental in the founding of the Society for the Relief of Poor Widows with Small Children in 1797. She loved her church, attended regularly, and was considered to be a very spiritual woman.

Unfortunately, the family business went bankrupt in 1800 and, three years later, William died of tuberculosis. Prior to his death, Elizabeth and William had traveled to Italy, seeking a cure. There, Elizabeth met Antonio Filicchi, who introduced her to Roman Catholicism. Elizabeth felt so drawn to the Church that she converted on March 14, 1805. She moved with her children to Baltimore, Maryland, in 1808 and established a school for girls, which later became

Saint Joseph College. One year later, she took her vows as a Sister of Charity of Saint Joseph. From Baltimore, she moved to Emmitsburg, where she eventually set up six branches of Mother Seton's Daughters to perform social work. She is also credited with laying the foundations for the American Catholic school system.

A typical day for Mother Seton would be "In the chapel at six until eight, school at nine, dine at one, school at three, chapel at six-thirty, examination of conscience and Rosary . . . and so it goes day after day without variation."[7] She was much loved by the sisters for her humor and compassion—sometimes, as the head of her community, she would call herself Mother Goose.

Elizabeth Seton died of tuberculosis on January 4, 1821, a day now celebrated in the Roman calendar as the feast day of the first American-born saint. She was forty-six years old. The sisters saved all her meager belongings, just in case the process for sainthood was ever put into motion.

In 1907 Cardinal Gibbons of Baltimore introduced the cause for the canonization of Mother Seton. Her writings were gathered and the local trials began. It was not until 1925 that the trials' findings were sealed and sent to Rome. Things progressed very slowly at the Congregation of Rites, which finally declared in 1936 that there was no obstacle to taking up the cause. Back in the United States, a buzz of activity continued: fund-raisers, speeches, and prayers to Mother Seton for healing miracles. By the time she was declared heroic and the title "venerable" was conferred, there were documented miracles ready for her beatification.

But miracles take a long time to verify. The Church interviewed witnesses to the healings of Sister Gertrude, a Sister of Charity, and of Ann Theresa O'Neill, both of whom attributed their cancer cures to be a direct result of praying to Mother Seton. It wasn't until March 17, 1963, that Mother Seton was beatified and given the title "blessed." Now, another two miracles had to be proven.

In the fall of 1963, a Lutheran man named Carl Kalin was diagnosed with a form of meningitis. The doctor thought he would live only for an hour or two. A relic of Mother Seton was applied to Kalin's body and prayers begun. Contrary to the doctor's prognosis, Carl Kalin lived, went back to work, and eventually converted to Catholicism. His cure was proclaimed a miracle. Pope Paul VI waived the requirement for a second miracle, and on September 14, 1975, Mother Seton became Saint Elizabeth Ann Seton.

Special services are held on major anniversaries of her feast day at the Chapel of Saint Joseph's Provincial House of the Daughters of Charity in Emmitsburg, the headquarters for her order of nuns, and at Trinity Episcopal Church in New York, where she was a member in her youth.

CHAPTER THREE

HOW DO SAINTS LIVE?

Teach us, good Lord, to serve Thee as Thou deservest; to give and not to count the cost; to fight and not to heed the wounds; to toil and not to seek for rest; to labor and not to ask for any reward, save that of knowing that we do Thy will; through Jesus Christ our Lord. AMEN.

—Saint Ignatius of Loyola
(16th century)

At some point in time in their lives, most Christian saints chose to dedicate their lives to God, following in the footsteps of Jesus. Some led lives of complete poverty, others were literally "soldiers" of God. Most, if not all, spent a great deal of time in prayer and meditation. They decided on different professions to serve mankind—they were missionaries, nurses, social workers, and scholars. Through their work for God, they serve today as examples of virtue and piety, love and patience, grace and understanding. Some saints were given the ability to perform miracles through God. Their lives on earth are shining examples to us as we aspire to heaven.

ARE ALL SAINTS MARTYRS?

In the early Church, almost all saints were martyrs, meaning that they were killed or executed for their beliefs. The Romans had extended their empire to most of the known world, bringing with them a law called *Pax Romana*, or the Peace of Rome. One aspect of the *Pax* decreed that all conquered nations demonstrate *pietas*, a mixture of fear and love that children were to show to their parents; parents, to the state; and all of society, to the Roman gods. When that happened, the Romans believed, the world would be at peace and the gods would nurture the empire.

But the Jews and later the Christians were a stubborn lot, refusing to bow down before the foreign gods. They were a thorn in the side of the Roman emperor. Those who spoke out against the Roman gods, spoke out against Rome. This was considered treason and had to be silenced. Christians had the unfortunate habit of proclaiming their faith in public, and thus were an early target for Rome. The apostle saints Peter and Paul were executed at this time, and the killings continued until A.D. 313.

After Emperor Constantine converted and issued the Edict of Toleration in A.D. 313, Christians were relieved from persecution. Now Christians were free to practice their religion, as many lived out their lives performing good works and deeds. Because martyrdom was on the decline, new qualifications for veneration by the Church came into place.

First, there were the confessors. These were men and women who confessed their belief in Christ at the peril of their lives, but were not afterward put to death. Instead, they may have been sentenced to penal labor or died in prison. One of the most famous of these was Saint Edward the Confessor, King of England. Next, the ascetics succeeded the martyrs as heroes of faith. Ascetics were usually monks who lived separate from society, in harsh environments with no possessions, and fasted often. Then there were the bishop saints, who were known for their influential activities, their writings, or their austere lives. Among them are Saint Gregory the Great and Saint Augustine of Hippo.

Originally, the Church had two distinct lists of saints: the *Depositio Martyrum* (the list of martyrs, which included confessors and ascetics) and the *Depositio Espiscoporum* (the list of deceased bishops). Eventually these lists became one.

TO BECOME A SAINT, DOES ONE HAVE TO BE AN ORDAINED MEMBER OF A CHURCH?

It gives one a huge advantage. Those deemed saints are most often martyrs or persons who have vowed to give their lives to God. One of the few exceptions was Saint Tarasius, a layman and chief secretary to Emperor Constantine VI. He was called to be the patriarch of Constantinople in A.D. 784, helping to restore holy images in churches. He died peacefully in the year A.D. 806, after having served as a patriarch for twenty-one years.

Many laypeople have also been canonized. Perhaps one of the most heartwarming stories of a non-ordained saint is that of Saint Isidore the Farmer.

Saint Isidore was born of poor parents in Madrid—he is now the patron saint of that city. As soon as he was old enough, he began working as a farm laborer on an estate outside the city. He and his wife had one son, but after he died, they agreed to live in celibacy. Saint Isidore spent his days in the field praying to God and talking with his guardian angel or the saints. He was known to spend Sundays visiting the churches in Madrid and sharing his meager meals with everyone, often leaving only scraps for himself. Four years after his death on May 15, 1130, his body was transferred to a shrine and reports of miracles began to spread.

WHAT IS A RULE?

Many saints founded religious communities, such as monasteries or convents, and each one had a set of regulations, called the rule, which was unique to that order. For example, the Poor Clares, when founded in Assisi, Italy, in 1212, was a rather severe community of nuns dedicated to meditation and prayer while suffering poverty and mortification.

Strictly speaking, there are four rules: the rule of Saint Basil (all monks of the East); the rule of Saint Augustine (Dominicans, Austin friars, Servites); the rule of Saint Benedict (Benedictines, Cistercians); and the rule of Saint

Francis (Poor Clares, all other friars). Carthusians, Carmelites, and Jesuits stand outside these four, as do some of the more recent institutions. Restrictions on the lives of the members can include diet (for example, vegetarian), seclusion, manual labor, and chastity.

WHAT IS A MIRACLE?

The word *miracle* comes from the Latin word *miraculum*, meaning a strange thing. We think of a miracle as an occurrence that contradicts the known laws of science and is, therefore, due to a supernatural cause or an act of God. A 1989 Gallup survey found that about 82 percent of Americans polled believed that "even today, miracles are performed by the power of God."[8]

Early Christians believed that saints had the ability to perform miracles both during their lifetimes and afterward. According to Luke 8:43-48, Jesus' followers, Jews and pagans alike, believed that God worked miracles through holy men, in this case through Christ himself:

> As he went, the people pressed round him. And a woman who had had a flow of blood for twelve years and could not be healed by anyone, came up behind him, and touched the fringe of his garment; and immediately her flow of blood ceased.
>
> And Jesus said, "Who was it that touched me?"
>
> When all denied it, Peter said, "Master, the multitudes surround you and press upon you!"

31

But Jesus said, "Someone touched me; *for I perceive that power has gone forth from me.*" And when the woman saw that she was not hidden, she came trembling, and falling down before him declared in the presence of all the people why she had touched him, and how she had been immediately healed. And he said to her, "Daughter, your faith has made you well; go in peace."

And, according to Acts 5:12-16, Christians believed that the mere shadow of Saint Peter falling on ill persons could cure them:

Now many signs and wonders were done among the people by the hands of the apostles. . . . The people held them in high honor. And more than ever believers were added to the Lord . . . so they carried out the sick into the streets and laid them on beds and pallets, that as Peter came by at least his shadow might fall on some of them. The people also gathered from the towns around Jerusalem, bringing the sick and those afflicted with unclean spirits, and they were all healed.

Many of the early martyrs performed miracles during their lives, but their powers seemed to become stronger after death, which the Church came to believe meant they were in heaven, closer to God. A saint's relic—whether it be a finger, a lock of hair, or an instrument of torture—is believed to be charged with the saint's energy and often seemed to cause a spontaneous healing upon contact.

In the early days of the Church, there was a sense of 'competing' between the miraculous powers of the Christians and those of the ancient pagan religions. It is said that the body of Saint Babylas (a bishop of Antioch who was martyred in

250 A.D.) was moved to Daphne (or Delphi) by the local churchmen to silence the power of the oracle of Apollo.

Saints not only could perform miracles, but like the pagan gods, their intercession could be invoked in specific, sacred places. And, like the pagan divinities, saints were assigned specific tasks and responsibilities. This continues today when we call upon, say, Saint Blaise to heal a sore throat, or Saint Antony of Padua to return a lost object.[9]

DO SAINTS PERFORM MIRACLES DURING THEIR LIFETIMES?

Not all saints perform miracles during their lives. In fact, some of the more famous saints—Saint Augustine, Saint Athanasius, Saint Gregory of Nyssa, and Saint Ignatius of Loyola—have never been credited with a miraculous event. As Saint Augustine once wrote, "It is a far better thing to convert a sinner than to restore a dead man to life."

But there have been others who did work miracles in their lifetimes. In 1121, Bernard of Clairvaux restored the power of speech to a dying man so that he could confess his sins. It was said that people were cured instantaneously when Saint Bernard made the sign of the cross over them.

Saint Francis of Assisi was given the gifts of both prophecy and miracles. He once met a man whose face was disfigured by cancer. Francis kissed the diseased man's face, healing him instantly. And in our own century, we have seen the cures wrought by Padre Pio of Italy.

WHICH SAINTS HAVE RECEIVED THE STIGMATA?

Two of the best-known saints who received the stigmata are Saint Francis of Assisi and Saint Catherine of Siena. The stigmata are bruises or bleeding wounds that appear on a person's feet, hands, side, or forehead. They represent the suffering of Christ on the Cross. Scientists are still at a loss to explain the documented cases of these marks.

The marks appeared on Saint Francis in 1224 after a forty-day fast and never left. He attempted to conceal them by covering his hands with his habit, and for the first time, he wore shoes and stockings. During the last two years of his life Francis suffered much pain and weakness from the stigmata, but he rejoiced in his discomfort. It was during this time that he wrote the *Canticle of Brother Sun*, perhaps one of his best-known works.

Saint Catherine of Siena received her stigmata after making her communion in the Church of Saint Christina, in Pisa, Italy. While she was in meditation before a crucifix, five blood-red rays appeared to emanate from it. The rays pierced her hands, feet, and heart, causing such intense pain that she fainted. These wounds remained all her life, invisible to all except herself. But when she died, they became visible to everyone. More recently, Padre Pio, an Italian monk, showed signs of stigmata throughout most of his life.

WHY DO SAINTS FAST?

The Roman Catholic Church distinguishes "fast" from "abstinence." A person who is fasting may eat only one full meal a day after the noon hour. The meal may or may not include meat. Drink is unlimited, but soup would be considered a meal. And fasting is only imposed as an act of penitence upon people who are over age twenty-one and under fifty-nine, in good health, and not engaged in heavy work. Abstinence, on the other hand, involves refraining from eating meat on certain days, and may include fasting as well. Abstinence is obligatory for all on Fridays, ember days (the Wednesday, Friday, and Saturday in a specified week of each of the four seasons), Ash Wednesday, the Wednesdays or Saturdays of Lent, before noon on Holy Saturday, and the vigils on the days before Pentecost, the Assumption, and Christmas.

Monasteries and convents were founded with rules for living. These included what and how often the members would eat. Fasting is a way of disciplining the body away from worldly pleasures, so that the penitent's soul might come ever closer to God. Saint Clare, the contemporary of Saint Francis of Assisi, founded convents in Italy, France, and Germany that observed perpetual abstinence from meat. The monks who lived with Saint Bernard of Clairvaux were served meals of coarse bread made from barley, and boiled beech leaves sometimes replaced vegetables. These two saints, among others, believed that their closeness to God resulted from their self-deprivation on earth.

WHY WERE MANY SAINTS HERMITS?

Going even further than those who fast, hermits feel that a complete withdrawal from the distractions and pleasures of the world allows them to contemplate God and rejoice in His greatness every moment of their lives.

The first and most famous of the hermit monks was Saint Antony the Abbot, who was born in Upper Egypt in A.D. 251. After hearing the words of Christ, "Go, sell what thou hast, and give it to the poor, and thou shalt have treasure in Heaven," (Mark 10:21), Antony gave away what he had and retired from the world. His only food was bread and water, eaten only after sunset. He founded several monasteries, which he visited occasionally, but he never stayed long, always returning to his mountaintop abode. When he did appear, people flocked to hear him preach and work miracles. He died in the arms of his two disciples, Macarius and Amathas, in his cell on Mount Kolzim near the Red Sea on January 17, A.D. 356. He was 105 years old.

ARE THERE ANY SAINTS WHO HELP SOLDIERS?

Saint George is widely loved for his tales of battle and knighthood, and several groups have claimed him for their own. He is the patron saint of England and of the Coptics

(Egyptian Christians). Muslims call him El Khuds ("The Holy") and identify him with the Prophet Elijah.

In 1098, Saint George was seen helping the Franks at the Battle of Antioch, and during the crusades, the shining specter of Saint George was reported fighting on horseback for the English. King Richard the Lion-Hearted of England prayed for his help before the Battle of Acre in 1190, and, sure enough, Saint George appeared on his white warhorse and led the troops to victory. More recently, in the Battle of Mons during World War I, British troops reported seeing Saint George come to their aid. English soldiers traditionally invoked Saint George before going into battle, as William Shakespeare wrote in *Henry V*:

> I see you stand like greyhounds in the slips,
> Straining upon the start. The game's afoot:
> Follow your spirit; and, upon this charge
> Cry "God for Harry! England and Saint George!"
>
> (3.1.31–34)

Saint George represents the ultimate triumph of good over evil, the white knight protector of the innocent.

WHY DID SAINTS PARTAKE IN WARFARE?
It would be idealistic to believe that Christianity spread soley on the basis of the Word of God. There have been times when feudal lords and kings decided to expand or consolidate their kingdoms, such as the Norman invasion

of England in 1066, or the establishment of the three Scandinavian countries of Denmark, Sweden, and Norway. Once the lands had been conquered, the rulers realized they needed an orderly state to maintain their positions. So they turned for their organized approach to the Church, which supported the royal authority by founding dioceses and monasteries. Saint Olaf of Norway was one ruler who did just that.

Olaf Haraldsson was the son of Harold Grenske, a Norwiegan lord, who succeeded in regaining most of Norway from the hands of the Danes and Swedes. He had already been baptised, and so he now set about converting his subjects. He imported a number of priests and monks from England. From these, he chose a priest named Grimkel to be his bishop and came to rely heavily on his advice. Unfortunately, King Olaf used excessive force to implement some of his new ideas and was eventually driven out of the country by his own countrymen, who were aided by King Canute of England and Denmark.

During an attempt to regain his kingdom, he was killed in the Battle of Stiklestad on July 29, 1030, and was buried by the Nid River, where he had fallen. Miraculously, a spring gushed out of the riverbank and became known for its healing powers. The following year, Bishop Grimkel ordered that Olaf was to be venerated as a martyr, building a chapel on the site. Eventually the Cathedral of Nidaros was built, dedicated to Christ and to Saint Olaf.

DID MANY SAINTS PARTICIPATE IN THE CRUSADES?

By the beginning of the eleventh century, the Muslims held the southern part of Spain, the Balearic Islands, Corsica, Sardinia, Sicily, all of coastal North Africa, Palestine, and part of Syria. What prompted the Church to advocate war against the infidel? History relates several possible reasons, including the desire to spread the Word of God and papal authority, and the attempt by means of the "Peace of God" to reduce feudal warfare, and perhaps to channel all this military energy against the Muslim Empire.

At any rate, European men took up the cause in great numbers, leading forces to regain the lost lands. As a result, a new type of monk emerged: the knight monk. These knights served as escorts for pilgrims to the newly liberated Holy Land and then stayed to continue fighting the Muslims. The first order, the Knights of the Temple, or the Templars, was established as a military religious order in 1128 when Saint Bernard of Clairvaux drew up a rule for them. They were soon followed by the Hospital of Saint John in Jerusalem, or the Hospitallers, and the Teutonic Knights.

Perhaps the most famous saint who was also a crusader was Saint Louis IX, King of France. He sailed on two crusades: one in 1248 and one in 1270. He experienced many adventures on his first crusade, including the invasion of Damietta, Egypt, and his capture by the Muslims. After his release and return to France in 1254, he was so distressed by the plight of Christians in the East that he continued to wear the cross of the crusaders on his clothes, indicating that he remained a crusader and intended to return to the Holy Land. In 1270, he landed in Tunis and contracted a fatal case of typhus. After his death on August 25, his heart and bones were taken back to France and enshrined in the abbey-church of Saint Denis. Louis was declared a saint in 1297.

DID ANY SAINTS DIE IN CHILDHOOD?

A few saints died in childhood. Saint Dominic Savio was only fifteen years old when he died, commenting on his deathbed about the beautiful things he saw in the afterlife. Saint Agnes was thirteen years old when she offered herself as a martyr rather than be married. The legend of Saint Tarcisius, the "boy martyr of the Holy Eucharist," states that he chose to die rather than give up the Sacred Host to some thieves. And there were the three Roman girls, the daughters of Saint Sophia. Saints Faith, Hope, and Charity were put to death during the reign of the emperor Hadrian when they were twelve, ten, and nine years old. Many believe that their story is a myth. One of the newest young saints is Saint Maria Goretti, whose purity touched the lives of all those who knew her.

Maria was born in 1890 near Ancona, Italy, to a farmer-laborer and his wife. Six years later, the family moved to Colle Gianturco, where Maria's father died of malaria. All the children pitched in to help their mother, and none was more helpful or cheerful than Maria. One day eleven-year-old Maria was at home mending a shirt when a neighbor named Alexander came into the cottage and attempted to rape her. When Maria protested vigorously, Alexander plunged a dagger into her back.

The young girl was rushed to the hospital, where she lived for another twenty-four hours. In her last moments, she offered forgiveness to her assailant and expressed concern about her mother. Eight years later, while in prison, Alexander had a dream about Maria that changed his life. When he was freed, his first act was to visit Maria's mother and beg her for forgiveness. Maria Goretti was canonized in 1950 by Pope Pius XII before the largest crowd ever assembled for a canonization.

ARE THERE ANY SAINTS WHO WERE OF ROYAL BLOOD?

During the Middle Ages, there were a number of royal saints. Just to name a few: Saint Henry, who became the Holy Roman Emperor in 1002; Saint Louis IX of France, who was the leader of the Seventh Crusade; Saint Edward the Confessor of England, who had the ability to cure scrofula, or tuberculosis of the lymphatic glands, by his touch; Saint Olaf of Norway, who helped to convert his nation; Saint Elizabeth of Hungary, who became a Franciscan after the death of her husband; and Saint Eric of Sweden, who established Christianity in Upper Sweden.

Perhaps one of the more interesting royal saints is Saint Wenceslaus of Bohemia, patron of Bohemia and the Czechs. He was raised as a Christian by his mother and, on becoming king of Bohemia, announced that he would support God's law and His Church. He signed a treaty with the German emperor, Henry I, recognizing him as his overlord, thereby preserving peace and Christianity for his subjects.

However, Wenceslaus's brother, Boleslaus, accused his brother of trading away Bohemia's sovereignty and decided to murder him. On September 28, A.D. 984, Boleslaus invited his brother to celebrate the feasts of Saints Cosmas and Damian with him. As Wenceslaus walked to church, he was killed by his brother and his friends, murmuring as he fell, "Brother, may God forgive you." King Wenceslaus was instantly proclaimed a martyr by his people, and pilgrimages to his shrine produced many miracles. We know him better today as "Good King Wenceslaus," the subject of the popular Christmas carol written in the nineteenth century by J. M. Neale.

HOW DO SAINTS HELP EVERYDAY PEOPLE?
Saints make no distinction between rich and poor, white collar or blue. They have shown throughout their lives their unconditional love for their fellow man, and there is no reason to believe that this quality leaves them at death. Padre Pio said that he would be able to help people more after he was dead. And the numerous healings that have occurred since then appear to vindicate his words. To those who humbly seek the help of the saints, they stand ever ready to be of aid.

I was reading a booklet I received from the shrine to Saint Anne at Saint Anne de Beaupré in Québec, Canada, and one story stood out among the many cases of Saint Anne's help. It was written by a mother to the keepers of the shrine:

> [My] child was born in 1981. When he was five months old, I realized he was not normal.... [I was informed that] he was a Mongolian child, who would have no teeth, no hair and would not be able to walk. I returned to my baby's room, held him in my arms and asked Saint Anne to help me take care of him. "He is mine," I kept repeating to myself. I felt like bursting into tears, but instead of crying, I gathered all my strength and smiled. The nurses, who had been watching me, remarked: "But, you don't understand . . . How can you be so calm?" . . . I retorted: "Even if my child is Mongolian, I will not be ashamed to say he is mine."
>
> I commended my child to Saint Anne in the awkward words of a person of low schooling. That day, I just spoke to Saint Anne as to my mother, asking her to make my other children and especially my sons and daughters-in-law accept this baby. I stayed a whole month at the hospital, giving medicine to my child, and sleeping on two chairs. I was afraid they would let my baby die.
>
> My child is now five years old. He walks, talks a little, has all his teeth and even attends the village school....Father, please bless the medal my baby will wear, and the rosary I will use to thank Good Saint Anne.[10]

CHAPTER FOUR

WHAT IS THE HISTORY OF SAINTS?

Take, Lord, all my liberty,
my memory, my understanding,
and my whole will.
You have given me all that I have,
all that I am,
and I surrender all to your divine will,
that you dispose of me.
Give me only your love and your grace.
With this I am rich enough,
and I have no more to ask. AMEN.

—Saint Ignatius of Loyola
(16th century)

Legends surrounding the history of saints are a mixture of fact and fiction. We know very little, if anything, about some saints. All we know about Saint George, for example, is that there was a George whose martyred remains were venerated in Syria from the fourth century. And the only fact we know about Saint Christopher is that a church was dedicated to him at Chalcedon, near Constantinople, in A.D. 450.

So how can we tell fact from fiction? During the Middle Ages, lives of the saints became embroidered with tales of amazing events and miraculous powers. Saints Cosmas and Damian are reported to have survived numerous execution attempts. It is said that they were drowned but that angels revived them; they were burned, but escaped unharmed; and they were stoned, but the stones boomeranged back upon those who had thrown them. Saint Roch was reported to have cured victims of the plague by making the sign of the cross over them. Saint Lucy is said to have pulled out her eyes to disfigure herself, thereby discouraging the advances of a suitor; but miraculously, her eyes were restored to her. One of the legends of Saint Sebald claims that he instructed a peasant woman to throw icicles on a dying fire on a cold winter's day when the fuel had run out. The woman did so, and the fire burned anew, warming the small hovel.

Some of the more recent saints left personal writings through which we can obtain a glimpse into their exemplary lives. Today, scholarly studies on the lives of saints, which date back to the beginning of the 1600s, focus largely on separating fact from fiction. Yet legends still exist, peppering the lives of saints with mystery and virtue.

WHO WAS THE FIRST SAINT?

Saint Stephen, whose feast day is December 26, was the first Christian martyr. His day is unique among saints' days in that no church service or devotional watch (vigil) is held the evening before. An old rhyme noted with eagerness:

> Blessed be Saint Stephen!
> There's no fast on his even!

During his life, Stephen was selected to address complaints from Greek Christians about the distribution of food to the needy. He later debated the Christian faith in synagogues with the Jewish leaders of the day, confusing and angering them with his challenge to their beliefs. The Rabbis persuaded witnesses to testify that Stephen had spoken blasphemously against Moses and the Law and sentenced him to death by stoning. Traditionally, it is said that among the prosecutors was Saul, who later became Paul the Apostle after his conversion. Stephen's martyrdom was a favorite topic for Renaissance painters, who depicted the stoning.

WHO WAS THE FIRST SAINT
TO BE PUBLICLY VENERATED?

Even though Stephen was the first Christian saint, he was not the first saint to be venerated. The first recorded case of veneration comes from the middle of the second century, with the death of Saint Polycarp at Smyrna. His fellow Christians recovered his body after his martyrdom and cherished his bones as "more precious to us than jewels, and finer than pure gold."[11]

On the anniversary of his death, the local church members would gather at his grave to pay him honor. And, indeed, they would take strength from Saint Polycarp and from each other, for none knew when it might be his turn to profess his faith in Christ before being executed.

WHAT IS THE HIERARCHY OF SAINTS?

There are nine orders, or types, of saints:

1. Virgins
2. Apostles
3. Martyrs
4. Confessors
5. Prophets
6. Patriarchs
7. The Chaste
8. The Married
9. The Penitents

Distinction between the orders was often depicted in medieval art by using different colors of halos to represent the character of the saint. Members of the first four orders, the most exalted of all, have halos of gold. Prophets and patriarchs, who were the saints of the Old Testament and knew the truth imperfectly, have halos of silver. The halo of the chaste is red; that of the married, green; and that of the penitents, blue.

WHO ARE THE FOURTEEN HOLY HELPERS?

The Fourteen Holy Helpers are saints who were commonly invoked during the Plague in the Middle Ages for their sensitivity and healing abilities. The best known of the Fourteen Holy Helpers are: Saint Sebastian, Saint George, Saint Erasmus (or Elmo), Saint Christopher, Saint Giles, Saint Denys, and Saint Catherine.

WHO ARE THE DOCTORS OF THE CHURCH?

This title has been given to approximately thirty saints who were known for their brilliant writings and their influence on Church doctrine. Among their ranks are such greats as Saint Augustine, Saint Bede the Venerable, Saint Gregory the Great, and Saint Thomas Aquinas.

Saint Teresa of Avila, the first female saint to receive the title, was declared a Doctor in 1970. She was a Carmelite nun in the sixteenth century whose writings and speeches influenced the Church of her day. The second woman to be so honored was Saint Catherine of Siena.

WHAT IS THE GOLDEN LEGEND?

The *Golden Legend* is the English translation of the Latin *Legenda Aurea*, written by a thirteenth-century Dominican, James of Voragine. It was first printed in English by William Caxton at Westminster in 1483 and was thus one of the first books published using the printing press.

The *Golden Legend* drew on the abundant literature of saints that had been compiled throughout the centuries—the most famous of which are perhaps the dialogues written by Saint Gregory the Great, who became pope in A.D. 590. The *Golden Legend* incorporated legends, tales of miracles, and imaginary stories with authentic accounts of the saints. Translated into many languages, it became enormously successful and can be found in most libraries even today.

WHO ARE THE BOLLANDISTS?

The Bollandists are a small group of men who are engaged in an astounding mission: to critically review the life of every saint, dismiss the fiction, and write an authoritative statement containing known facts. The Bollandists are members of the Society of Jesus and do their research in Belgium. Father Herbert Rosweyde, who lived in Antwerp, Belgium, began work on the project in the early 1600s but died in 1629 with nothing ready for the printer. His work was entrusted to Father John Bolland (from whence we get the name Bollandists), who, with two other men, continued the research. The work has been carried on ever since, halting briefly in the early 1800s with the suppression of the Society of Jesus during the French Revolution.

Father Bolland decided to publish the works, which he called *Acts of the Saints* (*Acta Sanctorum*), according to the dates of the saints' annual feast days, along with critical commentaries and notes. After fourteen years of work, he produced two volumes for January. By the early years of the eighteenth century, the lives of the saints had been published up until the end of June, with the October edition appearing in 1883. October alone has thirteen volumes! The end of November and the month of December are yet to be published. The Bollandists also publish a periodical review called the *Analecta Bollandiana*, which first appeared in 1882, and update the previous volumes of the *Acts of the Saints* with newly canonized saints.

WHAT IS HAGIOGRAPHY?

Hagiography is the study of the lives of saints. It began in the 1500s as a direct answer to the criticism of the Protestants that veneration of saints was a form of idol worship. Much of the work has been done by the Bollandists, but the fascination of the lives of saints has attracted scholars from many backgrounds: history, folklore, and literature. The goal of all these researchers is to unravel the true historical lives of the saints and discard the hearsay.

WHAT IS THE ROMAN MARTYROLOGY?

The Roman Martyrology is the official listing of saints as recognized by the Roman Catholic Church. It is more commonly called the Roman calendar. In this document, the saints are listed chronologically by their feast days. Also listed is the location where their cults originated, what each saint did during his or her lifetime, and how they died.

The list started with the compilation of local church records and was copied and recopied through the centuries. Finally, in the eighth century, the English scholar Saint Bede (known to us as The Venerable Bede) added a short history of the life and death of the saint to each entry. Throughout the years, others added to the Martyrology until Pope Gregory XIII decided to compile an official edition. This work was completed in 1584. It has been reedited many times throughout the centuries, with corrections made and recently canonized saints added. Today it is kept at the Vatican in Rome, in a large book that includes the names of all the saints recognized by the Roman Catholic Church.

Of course, there are also the local martyrologies or calendars. The Roman Catholic Church has authorized local veneration of the saints listed, and they appear in a supplementary listing to the Roman Martyrology.

WHAT IS THE CHURCH CALENDAR?

In the early days, each local church had its own calendar or martyrology for remembering its own martyrs and recording the place and date of meeting to honor them. The calendar at Rome was quite extensive and became known as the *Depositio martyrum*. Here's a sample entry:

> January 20th: anniversary of Fabian — at the cemetery of Callistus; and of Sebastian, at the Catacombs.

Later the church at Rome began to include the martyrs of other churches and inserted the names of the Apostles and Saint Stephen into the records. Around the end of the fourth century or the beginning of the fifth, a feast commemorating the Virgin Mary appeared.

Today, there are many church calendars. The Roman Catholic Church has one official listing which includes a list of saints to be venerated worldwide. Local churches have their own lists, consisting of saints particular to their region, including their patron saints. The Church of England has its own calendar, as does the Anglican Church in Canada and the Episcopalian Church in the United States.

HOW MANY SAINTS ARE THERE?

The answer to this question really depends on how the word *saint* is interpreted. *Butler's Lives of the Saints* lists more than 3,000, and these volumes are by no means exhaustive! The Bollandists' *Acts of the Saints* mentions that there are about 20,000 saints, and from there, the sky's the limit.

If we define saints as people who have led exemplary lives, then just about all of us know or have known someone who is a saint, even if they haven't been canonized by the Roman Catholic Church. And there are certainly many quiet Mother Teresas and Gandhis who work behind the scenes doing charitable acts for their fellow humans.

HOW MANY NORTH AMERICAN SAINTS ARE THERE?

Many North American saints were early Jesuit missionaries to the Native Americans. The Native Americans called them Blackrobes after their black garments. There were eight fathers: Jogues, Brébeuf, Lalemont, LaLonde, Chabanel, Garnier, Goupil, and Daniel, all of whom are martyrs. Of these Blackrobes, Saint Jean de Brébeuf is perhaps the best known for writing the hauntingly beautiful "Huron Carol." Saint Jogues and his companions were canonized in 1930 and declared the patron saints of North America. Their shrine is located in Midland, Ontario, Canada, near the original Christian settlement of Saint Marie. The settlement had been abandoned in 1650 due to constant Iroquois attacks. It was during one of these Iroquois attacks on the Huron Indians that Fathers Daniel, Lalemont, Brébeuf, and Jogues were killed.

The United States can boast of three American saints: Saint Frances Xavier Cabrini, Saint Elizabeth Ann Seton, and Saint John Neumann. Saint Frances Xavier Cabrini, best known as Mother Cabrini, and Saint Elizabeth Ann Seton were both nuns who dedicated a great portion of their lives to the betterment of others. Mother Cabrini was not born in the United States but spent a good deal of her life in New York City and eventually become a naturalized American citizen. Mother Seton was born in New York City and lived near Baltimore, Maryland, where she is lovingly remembered today for the work she did for the poor.

January 5 is the feast day for Saint John Neumann, who was born in Bohemia and ordained to the priesthood in 1836 in New York. He died in 1860 after having served as bishop of Philadelphia for eight years. He was canonized in 1977.

One of the newest Canadian saints is Marguerite Bourgeoys (canonized in 1982), who opened the first school in Montréal (then called Ville Marie or City of Mary) in 1658. In 1675, she founded the chapel of Notre Dame de Bon Secours, a place of pilgrimage for devotion to Mary. It was under her direction that one of the wooden crosses placed on Mount Royal was erected. These are the forerunners of the famous cross which stands on Mount Royal today overlooking the city of Montréal.

WHO WAS THE FIRST AMERICAN SAINT?

The first American to become a saint was Mother Cabrini. She was born at Sant' Angelo di Lodi, in Lombardy, Italy, on July 15, 1850. During her confirmation at the age of seven, she fell into a trance-like state. When she came to, she had a newly found determination to become a missionary.

Toward the end of the nineteenth century, Italian emigration to America was growing rapidly. Immigrants in New York, Chicago, and other cities were living under terrible conditions. When the news reached the Vatican, Pope Leo XIII decided that an order of Italian nuns would help alleviate their suffering. So he sent Mother Cabrini to New York, along with the order of Missionary Sisters of the Sacred Heart, which she had founded in Italy. At Saint Joachim's Church in New York's Little Italy, the order set up shop, caring for homeless children. Because they were often financially strapped, they begged for money while carrying large baskets to collect food. By the time of Mother Cabrini's death on December 22, 1917, the order had established sixty-seven charitable foundations. Mother Cabrini's advice to her nuns remains timeless: "Difficulties are children's toys. Imagination is what makes them big."

Soon after her death, the study for the Cause of Beatification was begun. At the request of the pope, the usual fifty-year waiting period after a person's death was waived, and Mother Cabrini was declared blessed on November 13, 1938. It was the first time in history that a cardinal celebrated both the funeral services and the beatification ceremonies for the same person. Eight years later, she was proclaimed Saint Frances Xavier Cabrini. Her feast day of November 13 is celebrated at Mother Cabrini High School in New York City, where she is buried in the chapel.

ARE THERE ANY CANONIZED SAINTS FROM NON-EUROPEAN CULTURES?

Most of the saints we know of are European. But with the spread of Christianity, a number of martyrs from distant countries have arisen. Some of the earliest were Japanese and had been converted to Christianity by Saint Francis Xavier and his disciples. Saint Paul Miki, a Japanese nobleman who had become a Jesuit preacher, was martyred, along with nineteen others, near Nagasaki in 1597. They were all canonized in 1862.

Christians in Korea suffered persecutions from 1791 until 1886. Among the many who died was Saint Andrew Kim, the first Korean-born priest. There were also many Christian martyrs in Vietnam. Saint Andrew Dung Lac, a Vietnamese priest, was beheaded in 1839.

The first Catholic missions to central Africa were established in 1879 by a group called the White Fathers. After making some progress in Uganda, they met up with a local ruler by the name of Mwanga, who was determined to rid his people of Christianity. Mwanga became angry when one of his subjects, Joseph Mkasa, a native who had converted to Christianity, reproached him for his debauchery with young boys. The ruler systematically killed native Ugandan Christian priests, who were instructing the people in the ways of Christ, and young boys who refused to service the king's desires. Among the many who died were Saint Joseph Mkasa, Saint Charles Lwanga, Saint Matthias Murumba, and Saint Andrew Kagwa. These men, along with eighteen others, were canonized in 1964.

WHAT EFFECT DID THE PROTESTANT REFORMATION HAVE ON SAINTS?

The Protestant Reformation in the 1500s had a huge effect on the cults of saints. One of the best-known critics of the Roman Catholic Church was the German Protestant Martin Luther, who felt that the veneration of saints was idolatrous and pagan in its origins. He believed that saints could not serve as intermediaries between man and God, and that the lives of saints had been embroidered with many layers of fiction and legend. However, Martin Luther didn't completely dismiss the idea of sainthood. He did believe that the lives of saints held a special place in Christian spirituality:

> Next to Holy Scripture there certainly is no more useful book for Christians than that of the lives of the saints, especially when unadulterated and authentic. For in these stories, one is greatly pleased to find how they sincerely believed in God's Word, confessed it with their lips, praised it by their living, and honored and confirmed it by their suffering and dying.[12]

In order to answer some of the Protestants' criticism, Church scholars began to look at the life of each saint and weed out fiction from facts. And their work has continued to this day. In 1969, the Church deleted from the calendar fifty-two saints whose existence had been questioned, and ninety-two others were only granted optional feasts.

WHO ARE SAINT THOMAS'S CHRISTIANS?

We don't know a lot about the Apostle Thomas, the "doubting Thomas" of the New Testament. Legend has it that he was sent to preach the Gospel in India in the year 53 A.D. and was martyred there at the hands of the king Mylapore. The cathedral of San Thomé marks his burial place and every year, pilgrims visit his shrine on Saint Thomas's Mount.

The Christians of Malabar in south-west India claim to be descended from Brahmans (the highest Hindu caste) who were converted by Saint Thomas himself. They are called Saint Thomas's Christians.

CHAPTER FIVE

WHAT ARE THE CULTS OF SAINTS?

God the Father of our Lord Jesus Christ, increase us in faith and truth and gentleness, and grant us part and lot among His saints. AMEN.

—Saint Polycarp (1st century)

The word *cult* comes from the Latin *cultus,* which means care or cultivation. The word later evolved to its present meaning: a system of religious worship of or excessive admiration for a person or idea. In the Roman Catholic sense, the word means the honoring of a saint by public acts.

The cults of saints began in the second century A.D. as honors were paid to the first Christian martyrs during their deaths and burials. The early Christians believed that nothing was more desirable than to die for Christ. The faithful collected the remains of the martyred for burial, celebrating the burial or *depositio,* saying it was a martyr's birthday into a life of blessedness. The local church would congregate every year on this happy occasion and celebrate the Eucharist, during which the martyr would be honored.

In doing this, the Christians were taking advantage of pagan Greco-Roman customs in order to disguise their own ceremonies. The Greeks and Romans greatly respected burial grounds and would even divert roads around an old cemetery. They would meet at the grave sites of their ancestors and hold commemorative rites celebrating the anniversary of their births.

At first, Christians performed their rites discreetly, but as the Church grew and persecutions lessened, the ceremonies were held openly, and more people came—often on pilgrimages—to celebrate. To accommodate them, and to add weight to the ceremonies, basilicas (from the Greek *basil,* meaning royal) were constructed over the tombs. Today, when people travel to visit the burial site of their favorite saint, they are simply following the early Christian tradition—the *cultus* of a saint.

WHAT ARE PILGRIMAGES?

You may be familiar with these verses from Geoffrey Chaucer's *Canterbury Tales:*

> Whan that April with his showres soote
> The droughte of March hath perced to the roote, . . .

Thanne longen folk to goon on pilgrimages,
And palmeres for to seeken straunge strondes
To ferne halwes, couthe in sondry londes
And specially from every shires ende
On Engelond to Canterbury they wende,
The holy lisful martyr for to seeke
That hem hath holpen whan that they were seke.

(verses 1-2; 12-18)

Chaucer, a fourteenth-century English poet, is telling us that springtime brings forth longing in people to go on pilgrimages, some to seek out far-off shrines in strange lands. Pilgrims come from every part of England, winding their way to the shrine of the martyr, Saint Thomas à Becket, who was murdered in Canterbury Cathedral in 1170.

In the Middle Ages, hardships on the pilgrimages were considered an essential part of the spiritual journey. Now, as in the days of Chaucer, people go on pilgrimages to seek the holy. Sometimes they are undertaken as a penance, as humble requests for healing, or as a temporary release from everyday living. Pilgrims visit holy shrines where a relic of a saint is kept. In England, during medieval times, the most famous national shrine was at Canterbury.

HOW DID PILGRIMAGES HELP SPREAD THE CULTS OF SAINTS?

Pilgrimages were, and still are, times of great adventure. A pilgrim met many other people on the road, some from different parts of the country and some from faraway lands. News traveled quickly about other saints and their shrines. As healings occurred, some would decide to go further afield in search of a miraculous cure or an answer to a prayer.

The Church did its part as well, by promoting the cults of new saints. New saints meant new shrines. And new shrines meant more pilgrims, who, like the tourists of today, spent money at the shrine and boosted the economy of the region.

HOW DID VENERATION OF SAINTS SPREAD THROUGH MEDIEVAL EUROPE?

Not only did the Church encourage the spread of veneration of saints by the use of festivals and preaching, but the cults also spread through word of mouth. The lay public were eager for news of wonder. Someone would claim a miracle in the name of a saint, and soon pilgrims would flock to the site. But individuals also played a part.

Parish priests did much to establish cults and influence followers. For example, Sir Christopher Trychay was a newly appointed parish priest of the village of Morebath, England, in 1520. He donated to the church a painted and gilt statue of Saint Sidwell, an English saint who had a healing well and shrine at Exeter.

Sir Trychay encouraged his parishioners' devotion to Saint Sidwell, and they responded enthusiastically with gifts of jewelry, coins, beehives, and fleece. By the mid-1530s, the altar on which the saint's statue stood was referred to as Saint Sidwell's altar, and Saint Sidwell was declared to be the co-patron of the parish along with Saint George. People began to name their children after Saint Sidwell, and in 1558, the burial of a child by the name of Sidwell Scely was recorded in the parish register by Sir Trychay.[13]

WHAT ARE SOME OF THE MOST POPULAR CULTS?

The fifteenth and sixteenth centuries were the heyday for the cults of saints. Even today in England, after the destruction of the monasteries during the reign of Henry VIII and the Protestant Reformation, there are copious reminders of the common people's love for their saints. We can find drinking bowls and cups, lintels and gable ends engraved with their names. There are also numerous records of children named after favorite saints. And saints' images filled the churches. For example, the parish church at Faversham in Kent had four images of the Virgin Mary, as well as images of twenty-nine additional saints, such as Agnes, Anthony, Christopher, Erasmus, George, John the Baptist, Katherine, Mary Magdalene, Paul, and Peter.

Many of these saints' cults are still strong today. The most popular cult is that of the Blessed Virgin Mary, which is widespread around the world. Other popular cults include those of the early Apostles, Saint Peter, Saint Paul, and Saint Luke, and contemporaries of Jesus—Saint Joseph, Saint Anne, Saint John the Baptist, and Saint Mary Magdalene.

WHAT ARE TODAY'S MOST POPULAR PILGRIMAGE SITES?

As in the past, pilgrims today visit sites all over the world. In medieval times, the most popular sites were the shrine of Saint James the Apostle (Santiago de Compo-stela) in Spain, the Tomb of Saint Nicholas in Bari, Italy, the Shrine of the Three Holy Kings in Cologne, Germany, and the Sanctuary of Saint Mary Magdalene in Marseilles, France.

Of course today, one of the most favorite sites is the Holy Land, to retrace the steps of Christ at Easter, partake of celebrations at Christmastime, and to see many of the places mentioned in the New Testament. But shrines of the saints are still very popular destinations. Let's explore some:

SAINT PETER'S BASILICA, VATICAN CITY

The magnificent basilica of Saint Peter stands like a beacon within the city of Rome, on the grounds of the Vatican city-state. Thousands of tourists flock here each year from around the world, perhaps to celebrate Mass with the pope, to witness the canonization of a saint, or simply to see the wonderful treasures of the Vatican. But underneath all the grandeur lies the tomb of Saint Peter himself. If ones goes down into the grottoes, it is clear that the tomb was venerated in this exact spot as early as the second century. Although as many miracles are not attributed to this site as to some other pilgrimage sites in recent years, Saint Peter's is on the top of the list for Christian pilgrims.

LOURDES, FRANCE

Mention "pilgrimage" and most people think of Lourdes, France. At age fourteen, a young French girl named Bernadette began to see visions of the Virgin Mary at the grotto of Massabielle, beside the River Gave. Crowds of people began to join her at the site, and the vision instructed her to have a chapel built so that pilgrims might bathe in and drink from the spring that gushed out of the rock where the girl had dug. The last time the apparition appeared was on July 16, 1858, the Feast of Our Lady of Mount Carmel.

In 1864, Bernadette offered herself to the sisters of the convent of Notre-Dame de Nevers, and there she lived out the rest of her life. She had always been a sickly child and finally succumbed to her illnesses, dying on April 16, 1879. Thirty years later her body was taken out of its grave in the convent of Nevers and found to be in excellent condition. On December 12, 1933, Pope Pius XI proclaimed her Saint Mary Bernarda, better known to us by the pet name given her by friends and family, Saint Bernadette. Pilgrimages to the grotto at Lourdes continue today, spurred on by stories of miraculous cures.

FÁTIMA, PORTUGAL

A more recent site for pilgrimage, Fátima is the site where three children, Jacinta, Lucia, and Francisco, had six visions of Our Lady of the Rosary in 1917. They were told by the Lady that a miracle would happen that October in order to convince people of the truth of their visions. On October 13, after the Lady revealed herself to be the Lady of the Rosary to the children, she rose heavenward and opened her hands. The light from them shone like the sun, and the crowd that had assembled then witnessed the "Miracle of the Sun": The sun appeared to revolve on itself, sending out a colored spectrum that reflected on the ground and on the people. It then seemed to leave the sky and hurtle down toward the earth.

The "sun dance" was reported in the local newspapers, and people began to flock to the site. Miracles began to happen, and a new pilgrimage site was established with thousands of visitors each year. Two of the children, Jacinta and Francisco Marta, currently have cases for canonization under consideration.

SAINTE ANNE DE BEAUPRÉ, CANADA

Saint Anne's basilica at Beaupré, Québec, Canada, is one of the largest and most beautiful churches in North America. And some say that as a place of healing and pilgrimage, it is second only to Lourdes. How did this come about?

In the 1650s, a ship from Brittany bound for the New World began to founder in a storm. Those aboard said that if they were spared, they would build a chapel to Good Saint Anne. Anne was the mother of Mary, the Mother of Christ. The crew did arrive safely, and in 1658 a chapel was built. The story goes that one of the workmen, Louis Guimont, a man crippled with rheumatism, experienced a miracle at the work site. After laying three of the foundation stones, Louis discovered he could stand up straight and cried out that he had been cured! News spread and, down through the centuries, more and more pilgrims began to visit the site, reporting other healing miracles. In September 1984, the site was visited by Pope John Paul II, who like millions before him, prayed at the foot of the "Miraculous Statue" of Good Saint Anne. Today, it is a popular place for both pilgrims and tourists alike.

WHAT ARE RELICS?

Simply put, relics are primarily the actual bodily remains of saints and instruments of their penance, suffering, and death; and secondarily, objects that had some contact with their bodies or graves. A relic can be anything from a saint's finger to a piece of clothing worn by a saint during burial. The early Church believed that grave sites should not be disturbed, so basilicas were often built over the tombs. For instance, Saint Peter's Cathedral at the Vatican is situated over the burial place of the Apostle Peter.

As a saint's cult spread, relics were dispersed far and wide. It soon became very difficult to control the genuineness of relics, which were in great demand and often stolen. Many people were taken in by unscrupulous traders who hawked items they claimed to be authentic relics. Chaucer tells us about a corrupt pardoner (a person who dispensed papal pardons for sins in exchange for contributions) in his fictional pilgrimage account, *Canterbury Tales*:

> He hadde a crois of laton, ful of stones,
> And in a glas had hadde pigges bones,
> But with thise *relikes* whan that he foond
> A poore person dwelling upon lond,
> Upon a day he gat him more moneye
> Than that the person gat in monthes twaye. . . .

(verses 701–706)

The pardoner apparently sold pigs' bones as saints' relics to poor, unsuspecting persons who were living in the countryside. He made quite a bit of money in the bargain—two months of that person's wages!

Today, as in the past, relics are a very important part of the veneration of a saint. In fact, a small relic is sealed into the stone table of every new altar when the bishop consecrates it.

WHICH SAINTS' RELICS ARE THE MOST FAMOUS?

While we cannot be certain about the authenticity of some of the older relics—such as part of the forearm of Saint Anne at Sainte Anne de Beaupré and even the relics of Saint Peter claimed by the Vatican—faithful pilgrims still visit the shrines. Perhaps some of the most famous relics that exist today are:

* Holy shroud of Turin, reported to be the winding cloth of Jesus when he was laid in the tomb;
* Veil of Veronica, which is preserved in Saint Peter's in Rome and may only be handled and exposed for veneration by a canon of the basilica;
* Veil of Our Lady, given by Charlemagne to Aix la Chapelle and preserved in the cathedral of Chartres;
* Relics of Saint James the Great, miraculously revealed in the 9th century and preserved in Santiago de Compostela, Spain.

The true Cross of Jesus was found by the Empress Saint Helen in about 318 and soon portions of it had spread around the known world. In England today, there is a small piece of it enclosed in the cross on the bell tower of Westminster cathedral. The Crown of Thorns which was placed on the head of Jesus is said to be preserved in Notre Dame in Paris. It no longer contains any thorns, as these were given away by Saint Louis, King of France, in golden reliquaries (a reliquary is a vessel for holding a relic). One of these reliquaries is on display at the British Museum, London.

WHICH SAINTS' RELICS HAVE BEEN REPORTED MISSING OR STOLEN?

Theft of relics was commonplace both by robbers looking for resale value and by clergy who wished to obtain relics for their own parish. In 1177, Saint Petroc's relics were stolen from a monastery in Cornwall, England, and presented to the abbey of Saint-Meen in Brittany. King Henry II intervened to get them back. In Agen, France, a monk of Conques kicked in the side of Saint Faith's shrine and carried off the relics in a sack.

Theft of relics didn't just happen in the Middle Ages. Less than a year after the funeral of Saint Teresa of Avila, her tomb was opened and Father Gracián, the Father Provincial, cut off her left hand, keeping for himself the little finger. "When I was captured by the Turks they took it from me, and I redeemed it for about twenty reals and some gold rings," he wrote.[14]

WHAT ARE VOTIVE OFFERINGS?

What a beautiful sight it is to walk into a church and see the flickering candles light up a chapel! The ritual of lighting a votive candle is a form of thanking a saint for favors rendered. Because it consumes itself, the candle represents a type of sacrifice, just as incense, with its fragrant, rising smoke, is symbolic of prayer. In the Middle Ages, grateful people would often "measure themselves" to their saint by setting a candle of their own height and weight before a statue or painting of the saint who had granted a favor.

Lighting a candle before the image of a saint is just one of the ways people thank saints. In the Church of the Assumption in London, silver hearts are offered; at Westminster Cathedral, wedding rings; and at the shrine at Lourdes, surgical instruments. It really doesn't matter what you offer, just as long as your offering is sincere.

WHAT ARE MIRACLE PLAYS?

Miracle, or mystery, plays were popular during the Middle Ages, especially with the common people. The plays dealt with the lives of the saints, emphasizing good Christian lifestyles, and were usually performed outdoors on temporary stages. They often played a large part in acquainting the public with the lives of the saints. Unlike the passion plays, which deal with the last days of Jesus, the revival of miracle plays has not, as yet, been successful.

WHY ARE SAINTS DEPICTED WITH HALOS?

Halos (also known as aureole, glory, or nimbus) have been used by painters and sculptors for centuries to depict revered, sacred, or holy people. Before the time of Christ, halos were used to show the dignity and power of people such as emperors. In the centuries after the death of Christ, even Satan was sometimes pictured with a halo to symbolize the power he wielded. By the sixth century, halos were used solely to depict holy or saintly people.

Halos come in all sizes and shapes. Early painters portrayed a saint after death with a circular halo around the head. If the saint was portrayed before death, the halo would be painted in the form of a square. And if a saint was pictured ascending to heaven, an oblong radiance of light, called a glory, surrounded the entire body of the saint. As we have already seen, most often the halo is gold. A red halo symbolized not only the chaste, but also saints with zeal and passion. Judas is sometimes depicted with a black halo, symbolizing his ultimate rejection of God.

It is interesting to note that the disc-shaped, golden halos that can often be seen behind saints' heads in paintings were derived from statues of saints. In the early centuries, statues were erected outside and metal discs were fastened to the heads as a form of protection from the weather. Today, the

Catholic Church has ruled that people cannot be depicted with a halo in official Church art unless they have gone through the canonization process and have been duly declared a saint by the pope.

WHY ARE SAINTS OFTEN PICTURED WITH CERTAIN OBJECTS?

Often artists would depict saints with specific items that symbolize a saintly act that serves as an example of their piety or holiness. For example, Saint Francis of Assisi is frequently set among friendly beasts, which signifies his patronage of animals. Saint Mary Magdalene is widely known and revered for anointing Jesus' feet with oil; she is portrayed with a box of ointment. Saint Nicholas is shown with three golden balls to represent the three bags of gold that he gave to the daughters of a poor man, thus saving them from the fate of prostitution. Saint Sebastian was shot with arrows as punishment for converting others to Christianity, but lived to reproach his tormenters. He was then beaten to death with clubs, and his body was thrown into the sewers of Rome. To symbolize his initial brush with death—and ironically, his patronage of archers—he often appears with his body pierced by arrows.

The early Christian Church also used the symbols of the cross and fish in order to identify other friendly Christians. Symbolism became an important part of later religious art. Here are a few additional symbols:

LAMB

The lamb symbolizes unblemished sacrifice, modesty, and innocence. A lamb at the feet of Saint John the Baptist illustrates his sacrifice; at the feet of Saint Agnes, her childlike innocence. Up until the sixth century, Christ was depicted as a lamb. But in A.D. 692, the Church decreed that the human face and form of Christ could be used in art for the symbolic Lamb of God.

DOVE

The dove is the emblem of the Holy Ghost and of the soul of man. Dying martyrs are shown with a dove leaving their lips, representing the soul's flight to heaven. With female saints, the dove denotes purity. It is frequently seen beside saints who were considered especially inspired, for example, Saints Ambrose, Augustine, and Gregory the Great.

SWORD

The sword, when given to a warrior saint like Saint George, represents his battles for the sake of humanity. But it can also symbolize a violent death, as does an ax, a lance, or a club.

CHALICE

The chalice is the mark of faith and is often shown with Saints Barbara and John. When there is a serpent in the chalice, it symbolizes wisdom.

WHY ARE CHURCHES NAMED AFTER SAINTS?

A Roman Catholic Church is named after the divine person, mystery, sacred object, or saint in whose name the church is blessed (or consecrated). The high altar in the church is consecrated by a bishop and must contain a relic, usually associated with the intended church name, or titular. If the church is named after a saint, the saint becomes its patron. But if a blessed is chosen, an exception granted by the pope or a member of his court, called an indult, is required. The feast of the titular must be celebrated in the church, and the feast of the titular of a cathedral is observed throughout the diocese.

Churches of other Christian faiths may also be named after saints, especially those of the Anglican, Episcopalian, Eastern Orthodox, and sometimes the Presbyterian and the United Churches. In the case of the Church of England, many Roman Catholic churches were taken over during the reign of Henry VIII and the time of the English Reformation. The Reformers dropped all the saints' feasts in the Roman Calendar except for those of the Apostles, the commemoration of the Holy Innocents (the children of the New Testament who were killed by King Herod), Saint Stephen, the Evangelists, Saint John the Baptist, All Saints, and Saint Michael and All Angels. The Church retained its own local calendar of English saints, but had no formal service for many of them. There is no official process for the naming of a church; the life of a saint may appeal to the parishioners, or the priest may have his own personal patron saint. But it is commonly understood that the church is put under the saint's patronage.

CHAPTER SIX

WHAT IS A PATRON SAINT?

May the strength of God pilot us.
May the power of God preserve us.
May the wisdom of God instruct us.
May the hand of God protect us.
May the way of God direct us.
May the shield of God defend us.
May the host of God guard us against the snares of evil
and the temptations of the world.
May Christ be with us.
Christ before us.
Christ in us.
Christ over us.

May Thy salvation, O Lord, be always ours this day and forever more. AMEN.

—Saint Patrick (5th century)

(Part of the Breastplate prayer believed to have been composed by St. Patrick to prepare for his victory over paganism in Ireland.)

In reading this book, you may feel more attracted to one saint than to another. If so, you may wish to put yourself under the protection or patronage of that saint, as friends and followers did during his or her lifetime. The saint will then act as your guide and intercessor with the heavenly court.

In Roman Catholicism, Church law stipulates that parents choose a name for their children that reflects who their patron saint is. If the parents do not do so, the priest must add a saint's name to the one the parents have chosen and enter both names in the baptismal register.

The Church also allows for all types of organizations to be placed under the patronage of saints. According to Canon 1278:

> If all be done in order, it is praiseworthy that saints should be chosen by nations, dioceses, provinces, associations, religious families, and other places or moral persons (i.e., corporate bodies) and that, if the Apostolic See confirms the choice, those saints should be their patrons.

DOES EVERYONE HAVE A PATRON SAINT?

You only have a patron saint if you choose one. In choosing one, you put your life under the protection of the saint, learn about his or her life and work, and try to live following your saint's example. In the Roman Catholic Church, you might also assume the name of your saint at confirmation, which is when you confirm the vows made by your godparents at baptism.

HOW DO I FIND OUT WHO MY PATRON SAINT IS?

The clue to finding out who your patron saint is may be in your name. Your parents chose a name for you at birth and, if you are Roman Catholic, your priest may have added the name of a saint. Find out if any of your given names correspond to that of a saint. And if you feel drawn to the life of any particular saint, you may wish to put yourself under that saint's protection.

HOW AND WHEN IS PATRONAGE ASSIGNED?

Once a group of professionals, an organization, or a country decides on a patron saint, they then apply to the Sacred Congregation for the Sacraments and Divine Worship to confirm their choice. If the saint has just been beatified and not canonized, then the pope must make a special exception, called an indult. One might even ask that two patron saints be assigned: a principal patron and a lesser patron. Once the Holy See agrees to the application, patronage is assigned. This is, however, a fairly recent development. In the past, patronage was usually chosen because the saint did something in his lifetime that related directly to the profession or organization. Here are some interesting examples:

ACCOUNTANTS: SAINT MATTHEW

Before Jesus asked him to become one of His disciples, Matthew was one of the most disliked men in the world—a tax collector. Based on his knowledge of money, both accountants and bankers name him as their patron.

ASTRONAUTS AND PILOTS: SAINT JOSEPH OF CUPERTINO

Astronauts and pilots claim Saint Joseph of Cupertino as their patron because of his ability to levitate. Called the flying friar, Saint Joseph was reported to have levitated more than seventy times during his seventeen years in the Franciscan house of La Grottella.

DENTISTS: SAINT APOLLONIA

Legend says that Saint Apollonia was a beautiful maiden who died as a martyr. During a riot, she was tortured by anti-Christians who extracted her teeth with pincers. She assured those who were around her when she died that she would help anyone who suffered with toothaches.

DOCTORS: SAINT COSMAS AND SAINT DAMIAN

It is said that Saints Cosmas and Damian, brothers of Arabian descent, were both practicing physicians. Once they converted to Christianity, they refused to accept payment from their patients. One unusual legend relates that the brothers amputated the leg of a European and then surgically attached one donated by a Moor, thus leaving the European with one brown leg and one white. Because of their skilled surgical techniques, they are claimed as patrons by surgeons, pharmacists, and even barbers.

FLORISTS: SAINT ROSE OF LIMA

The patron saint of florists is Saint Rose of Lima, who worked tending gardens in the early part of her life, and later lived a solitary existence in a garden hut. One of her emblems is, appropriately, a rose.

LAWYERS: SAINT IVO

Saint Ivo studied at both the universities of Paris and Orléans, before going on to practice civil and ecclesiastical law. His particular love was to defend the poor, but he would take on rich clients as well. By the time he was thirty, he was appointed diocesan judge. He became renowned for his fairness. He died in 1303, leaving a legacy of professionalism.

MUSICIANS AND SINGERS: SAINT CECILIA

The beautiful Saint Cecilia is the patron saint of music, musicians, and singers. A legend from the Middle Ages tells that an angel, enraptured by the music that Cecilia sang in her heart to the Lord, left heaven to visit her. The English poet John Dryden writes about her in *Alexander's Feast: An Ode in Honor of Saint Cecilia's Day*:

> At last divine Cecilia came,
> Inventress of the Vocal Frame;
> The sweet enthusiast, from her Sacred Store;
>   Enlarg'd the former narrow Bounds,
>   And added Length to solemn Sounds,
> With Nature's Mother-Wit and Arts unknown before.
> Let old Timotheus yield the Prize,
>   Or both divide the Crown;
> He rais'd a Mortal to the Skies;
>   She drew an Angel down.

(171-180)

NURSES: SAINT CAMILLUS DE LELLIS

Saint Camillus de Lellis at one point in his life wanted to be a Franciscan friar, but ended up caring for the sick. In 1585, he founded the Ministers of the Sick, who cared for people both at home and in the hospital. Camillus was the first person to insist upon fresh air, isolation of infectious patients, and nutritious diets. He died in 1614 and was canonized in 1746.

POETS: SAINT COLUMBA

Saint Columba, one of the best-known saints in Scotland and Ireland, was renowned as a poet and bard. As legend has it, he once drove away a wild boar simply through the power of word.

SCIENTISTS: SAINT ALBERT THE GREAT

An authority on physics, geography, astronomy, mineralogy, chemistry, and biology, Saint Albert the Great was one of the greatest scholars of the Middle Ages. He died on November 15, 1280, in the presence of his students at Cologne. Although beatified in 1622, he was not canonized until 1931, when he was declared patron saint of scientists.

Some of the more recently designated patrons are: Saint Francis of Assisi (in 1979) for ecologists; Saint Benedict (1964), Saint Cyril, and Saint Methodius (1980) for Europe; and Saint Michael the Archangel (1950) for police officers.

DO ANIMALS HAVE PATRON SAINTS?

If we can have patron saints, then why can't animals as well? In this case, we chose their patron saints for them, based on events that happened in the lives of the saints. Thus, Saint Francis of Assisi, because of his great love for the animals, is honored with the overall role of being the patron saint of the animal kingdom. Legend has it that he preached to the birds, who in turn showed their understanding of his sermons by flying away in the formation of a cross. He is also credited with taming a wolf that terrorized the town of Gubbio, Italy.

Saint Anthony the Abbot, who was born in Egypt in A.D. 251, also has an animal connection. He became known as the protector of domestic animals after it was rumored that he had cured beasts of the plague.

If your favorite pet is sick, then you might want to invoke Saint Beuno, the patron of sick animals. If you are concerned for wild animals, turn to Saint Blaise, who tended sick and wounded wild animals while hiding in a cave. The dog lovers among us can look to Saint Hubert of Liège, who is invoked against rabies; and if you're a beekeeper, look to Saint Ambrose for help. According to legend, when Ambrose was a child a swarm of bees settled on him, but left him unharmed.

DO PLANTS AND TREES HAVE PATRON SAINTS?
Unlike animals, plants and trees do not have patron saints. This doesn't mean, however, that they have no significance to saints. In fact, many artists use plants to represent certain aspects of a saint—for example, a lily signifies purity; a rose symbolizes love.

And, of course, people who work with plants and trees have put themselves under the patronage of the saint who represents their work. Gardeners invoke Saint Fiacre, who tilled the soil in his garden with his staff instead of a plough.

DO COUNTRIES HAVE PATRON SAINTS?

Just like organizations, countries put themselves under the protection of a saint. Nations may decide by popular acclamation which saint they wish to have as their patron. In some cases, the person who "discovered" the land chose a patron saint. In the latter case, the saint was probably a favorite of the explorer or the patron saint of his home region or country.

Here's a list of some countries and continents and their patron saints:

THE UNITED STATES OF AMERICA

The Blessed Virgin Mary was chosen to be the patron saint of the United States in 1846. In 1914, a project was launched to build a shrine to her honor in Washington, D.C., which is now known as the National Shrine of the Immaculate Conception. This shrine is one of the largest religious buildings in the world, with fifty-six chapels and seating for over six thousand persons. It also contains some of the largest mosaics in the world. More than one million people visit it each year.

CANADA

Canada has many patron saints. Saint Joseph, the husband of Mary (and also the patron saint of the Universal Church), and Saint Anne, the mother of Mary, were chosen early on in the nation's history.

When Samuel de Champlain landed at the head of the Saint Lawrence River in 1603, he claimed New France in the name of his king and chose Saint Joseph as its patron saint. Soon afterward in 1658, a shipwrecked crew built a shrine to Good Saint Anne on the shores of the Saint Lawrence River at Beaupré, and Anne became another of Canada's patron saints. Both of these saints are invoked for healing, and Canada's role in United Nations peacekeeping efforts is appropriately—and honorably—to promote healing between peoples. On October 16, 1940, Pope Pius XII declared that the eight Jesuit martyrs who were missionaries to the native people were also to be honored as national patron saints.

LATIN AMERICA AND SOUTH AMERICA

Saint Rose of Lima was born at Lima, Peru, in 1586. As she was growing up, she decided to take Saint Catherine of Siena as her patron and follow her model of life. As Catherine had cut off her long, beautiful hair so as not to attract men, Rose often rubbed her face with hot peppers to produce blotches on her skin. She worked during the day in a garden and at night doing needlework to bring in some extra money for her family. But when her parents insisted that she marry, she refused for nearly ten years before finally taking a vow of virginity.

Rose joined the order of Saint Dominic, residing alone in a little hut within the garden. She placed a silver band studded with little prickles around her head, much like a crown of thorns. It was not long before news of her piety and loving nature spread around South America. Her last days were tempered by a severe illness, which caused her much pain. She died in 1617 and was canonized by Pope Clement X in

1671. Saint Rose of Lima was the first native of the New World to be declared a saint.

ENGLAND

Saint George, the shining knight in white armor, was officially recognized as the Protector of the Kingdom of England by Pope Benedict XIV in the eighteenth century. But Saint George was beloved by the English long before then, his fame coming to England with the Normans in 1066. During the seventeenth and eighteenth centuries, his feast day was an obligatory holiday for English Catholics. England also claims Augustine of Canterbury and Gregory the Great as her patrons.

SCOTLAND

Saint Andrew is the best-known patron of Scotland, along with Saints Columba, Queen Margaret of Scotland, and Palladius. Saint Columba (or Colmcille) was born in Ireland around the year A.D. 521 and later became a deacon, preaching and founding monasteries. After a dispute with a rival clan, he and twelve companions moved to Scotland.

Columba continued his missionary endeavors to such a great extent that, for three-quarters of a century, Celtic Christians upheld Columban traditions in opposition to those followed in Rome, including a different date for Easter.

IRELAND

Ireland claims Saint Brigid, Saint Columba and, of course, Saint Patrick as her patron saints. Interestingly, Patrick was not born in Ireland but in Britain. When he was around age sixteen, Patrick was taken prisoner by pirates who took him to Ireland and sold him into slavery. About six years later, he escaped and, after an arduous journey, returned to Britain. Patrick later went back to Ireland as a bishop, spreading his faith and converting many Irish from pagan worship.

WALES

Saint David, the lone patron for Wales, is the only Welsh saint to be widely recognized by the Church. Said to be of royal blood, David's reputation as a preacher and miracle worker grew as he established over twelve monasteries, and he later was recognized as the leading bishop of Wales.

EUROPE

One of the patron saints of Europe is Saint Benedict, patriarch of Western Monks. He was born around the year A.D. 547 to a noble family at Nursia, Italy. He was sent to Rome for his education, but soon realized that the depraved ways of the great city revolted him, and he decided to live his life in solitude.

Withdrawing to a cave at Subiaco, he remained there for several years, drawing a number of young disciples who wished to emulate him. Benedict founded his first monastery there before leaving for Monte Cassino, where he built two chapels. Soon other buildings joined the original two, and the foundation of the most famous abbey in the world was established. His followers flocked there from around Christendom, and Benedict was visited by many Church officials who witnessed his sanctity, wisdom, and miracles. While Benedict lived at Monte Cassino, he set down the basis for his rule, which outlines a communal life of prayer, study, and work.

Poor and rich, young and old came to see the holy man. He was said to be able to cure the sick, raise the dead, and prophesy future events. In fact, it is believed that he notified his disciples of his impending death and told them to dig his grave. Six days later, he died standing upright in chapel, supported by his brothers, with his hands uplifted toward the skies. Considering the influence he had on the monastic movement, and Europe in general, it is no wonder he is Europe's patron, along with Saints Cyril and Methodius.

ASIA, AUSTRALIA, AND NEW ZEALAND

Australia, New Zealand, the East Indies, and China all claim Saint Francis Xavier as their patron saint. Saint Francis Xavier was a member of the first band of Jesuits, which was founded by Saint Ignatius of Loyola. In 1540, Saint Ignatius invited Saint Francis Xavier to join the first missionary expedition for the order. One year later, Saint Francis Xavier sailed around Africa to India. From there he went on to preach in many parts of the Far East, including Ceylon and Japan. One of his deepest desires was to reach China, then closed to foreigners, but he died before his dream could be realized.

Although he never visited China, Australia, or New Zealand, the profound influence that Saint Francis Xavier had on the Far East during his last eleven years of life is revealed by his patronages.

WHAT IS THE DIFFERENCE BETWEEN A NATION'S PATRON SAINT AND ITS APOSTLE?

Very often the patron saint (or one of the lesser patron saints) of a nation and its apostle are one and the same. A country's apostle is usually the first missionary who came to the country and was successful in converting the inhabitants. Saint Augustine of Canterbury is the apostle of England as well as one of its patrons. Saint Columba converted the Picts and, therefore, is also listed as a patron of Scotland.

WHY ARE SOME HOSPITALS NAMED AFTER SAINTS?

The word hospital comes from the Latin *hospes* (a guest) and, in the middle ages, came to mean a charitable institution for the care of the poor or sick. Hospitals were usually founded by religious men and women, called hospitallers, and aided the aged, pilgrims, and orphans as well as the infirm. Perhaps one of the best-known hospitallers is Saint John of God who opened a house to help the sick and poor of Granada, Spain, in 1540. This became the foundation for the Order of the Brothers Hospitallers.

Like other institutions, hospitals were put under the protection, or patronage, of a saint.

CHAPTER SEVEN

HOW DO I ASK A SAINT FOR HELP?

These things, good Lord, that we pray for, give us
Thy grace to labor for. AMEN.

—Saint Thomas More
(15th century)

It is really quite easy to invoke or "call" a saint to help your
cause. Early Christians frequently invoked martyrs and dead
relatives with small requests: "Here lies the faithful Gentian
in peace, who lived twenty-one years, eight months and sixteen days. Intercede for us in your prayers, for we know you
are in Christ."

Most people find the easiest way to talk to the saints is
through prayer. Whether short or long, prayers are funda-
mental in contacting the saints. The purpose of prayer is to
talk to God or the Divine, to relate to Him our deepest fears

and hopes. But sometimes the Divine seems a little far away, so we turn to others who have experienced the joys and fears of this life, who seem closer to us. Through the examples shown by the lives of the saint, we can learn how to conquer our failings.

The Roman Catholic Church teaches that God gives the saints the ability to hear and see our needs. So we ask saints for guidance or help by calling upon them during prayer. Though saints often serve as a communication link between us and God, our prayers to the saints do not replace our prayers to God. To distinguish between the two forms of prayers, the Council of Trent decreed that when praying to God, the proper address should be: "Have mercy on us, hear us . . . ," whereas to the saints, it should be: "Pray for us . . . "

Prayer doesn't have to be tedious! Some find the structured environment of church ceremonies very comfortable; others might want to try contemplating in a quiet woodland place. Whatever feels comfortable to you is suitable.

Include in your prayers a message, question, or plea to the saint of your choice. And then wait in a silent place for an answer. It may come to you in meditation or in the business of your daily life. But we know that all prayers are answered, even if sometimes the answer is not what we had hoped for.

HOW DO I DECIDE WHICH SAINT TO INVOKE?
There are several questions to ask yourself when deciding which saint to invoke. First of all, what is your need? Many saints have been assigned specific tasks. For example, if you

need help with family troubles, Saint Eustace is the saint who is normally invoked. You may find the following list helpful in this regard. Perhaps the request is career-related. There are many saints who are claimed as patrons for many ranges of professions (see Appendix II).

But you may be looking for a saint to generally watch over your life and act as a protector or a guide. For this, reading about the lives of the saints will help you choose one who feels the most appropriate for you. The concise edition of *Butler's Lives of the Saints* is a good place to start. You might want to begin with your name, find out if it's a saint's name, and discover if his or her life resonates with you. Or, find out which saint has a feast day on your birthday—a calendar of saints' feast days appears in Appendix I.

In any case, the most important thing is to determine which saint feels right for you. In the Roman Catholic Church, children take a confirmation name when they are confirmed, at around age twelve or thirteen. This is the name of a saint they have read about and chosen to help guide their lives. The saint they choose means something personal to them, is an inspiration or a comfort, and, above all, is their protector.

WHICH SAINT SHOULD I INVOKE FOR . . . ?
Here's a selection of topics for which you may want to ask a saint for help:

CANCER

Those suffering with the pain of cancer can call upon Saint Aldegonda, who died of breast cancer in A.D. 684. While a nun at Maubeuge, France, she showed great strength and patience while she suffered with her illness and is thus able to understand and help those of us today who are either stricken with the disease or know someone who is.

FEAR

If you have a specific fear, such as fear of snakes, you would invoke the appropriate saint—in this case, Saint Patrick. But for fear in general, you can turn to your own patron saint for his or her aid in helping you overcome it.

FLOODS

The martyrdom of Saint Florian in A.D. 404 involved being scourged, flayed, and drowned in the River Enns. Saint Florian can also be invoked by those who are in danger from fire.

HANGOVER

An herb that became known for its curative powers for headaches and for the effects of overindulgence grew around Saint Bibiana's burial site. So Saint Bibiana is invoked for speedy recovery from a hangover.

HEADACHE

Saint Stephen's stoning was presided over by the Apostle-to-be Saint Paul, according to legend. Saint Stephen's invocation against headaches became widespread during the Middle Ages, as the pain of being stoned to death is associated with that of headaches.

LONG LIFE

Saint Peter was called upon by Jesus to be the rock upon which He built His Church. Tradition has it that Saint Peter was martyred and buried in Rome. Saint Peter's Cathedral was built over his burial site. He is the guard at the pearly gates of heaven, and consequently, is invoked for a long life here on earth.

LOST KEYS

Because of her hard work as the servant to a wealthy family in Lucca, Italy, for forty-eight years, Saint Zita is the patron saint of servants. She is also invoked by those who lose their keys.

LOST PROPERTY

Saint Anthony of Padua, a contemporary of Saint Francis of Assisi, gained a reputation as a worker of wonders, which made him extremely popular both during and after his life. It is related that a young man once borrowed Anthony's Book of Psalms without asking and was forced to return it after receiving a frightening vision; hence the reason for Anthony's patronage.

PROMPT SOLUTIONS

Although his veneration is widespread, there is no evidence that Saint Expeditus ever lived. It is suggested that his patronage of problem-solving comes from his name—which means to expedite.

PROTECTION FROM EARTHQUAKES

Saint Gregory the Wonderworker is said to have had a hand in a number of miraculous events involving movement of earth, both before and after his death. During his lifetime, it is said that the statues to the emperors in Pontus, where he was bishop, fell to the ground during an earthquake, and he ordered them to be replaced by Christian images.

SICKNESS

Saint John of God spent his latter years taking care of the poor and sick in a hospital he established in Granada, Spain. In 1570, twenty years after his death, the Order of Hospitallers was founded in his name.

SORE THROAT

According to legend, Saint Ignatius of Antioch, who died in A.D. 107, was the little child Jesus put in the center of his disciples when He explained that receiving a child in His name was the same as receiving Himself. When Ignatius arrived in Rome, he was arrested and flung to the beasts. But he called out the name of Jesus ceaselessly until he died; therefore, he is called upon to heal sore throats.

TRAVEL

The legend of Saint Christopher begins with a man named Offero who offered his services to the devil. He eventually decided to become a Christian, when he saw the demon flee before a white cross. Offero's instructor in Christianity gave him the task of carrying people across a river. One night during a storm, a child requested passage and Offero complied, although the child grew heavier and heavier as he made the crossing. On the other bank, the child revealed himself to be Christ and renamed his bearer Christopher, meaning Christ-bearer.

CHAPTER EIGHT

WHAT IS A FEAST DAY?

From silly devotions
and from sour-faced saints,
good Lord, deliver us. AMEN.

—Saint Teresa of Avila
(16th century)

A feast day is, in most cases, the day on which a saint died. Memorial services are held on this day to celebrate the saint's passing into a life of blessedness with God.

Long ago, feasts and festivals were the highlights in the lives of the common people in pagan Europe. When the Christian missionaries arrived, they attempted to merge these pagan celebrations with saint's feast days to create holidays (or holy days) to be celebrated by all. Thus, festivals became religious holidays when commoners put aside their labors and celebrated a day of rest.

In England, for example, there used to be forty saints' feast days in the calendar—and up until 1830, the Bank of England closed on all of them! In addition, lesser saints' days were observed locally, and tradespeople would celebrate their own patron saint's day. By the beginning of the nineteenth century, some of the festivities had deteriorated into brawls, so the puritanical Victorians decided to do away with them. It was, after all, very uneconomical to allow workers so much free time! Now, instead of forty to fifty holidays a year, most workers in England and other countries have ten or less.

WHAT ARE THE MOST WIDELY CELEBRATED SAINTS' FEAST DAYS?

Probably the two most widely and joyfully celebrated saints' days in North America are Saint Valentine's Day and Saint Patrick's Day. Both of these feast days have a long tradition of festivities.

SAINT VALENTINE'S DAY—FEBRUARY 14

Saint Valentine's Day is widely celebrated as a day for expressing love. But Saint Valentine himself did not have much to do with lovers. Valentine was a holy priest who lived in Rome in the third century. During a roundup of Christians by the emperor, Valentine and a friend helped many Christians get away to safety. But Valentine himself was captured, tortured, and finally clubbed to death on February 14, A.D. 273.

The theme of Saint Valentine's Day most likely came from the ancient Roman festival of Lupercalia, which was celebrated on February 15 in honor of the goddess Februata Juno. Lotteries were traditionally held in which the names of all eligible young girls in the district were placed in an urn, and each boy drew the name of a partner. The idea was brought to Britain by the Romans, and—given that the two festivals were only a day apart—the love lottery merged with the celebration of Saint Valentine's feast day as many people converted to Christianity.

Love lotteries continued to be held until the beginning of this century. In aristocratic circles in the seventeenth century, people drew lots for a full year of pairing. Apparently some men were thankful when they drew the names of children and not women, as the women expected expensive gifts throughout the year.

The first commercial Valentine's Day cards appeared in England around 1800. In the United States, Miss Ester Howland created her own messages for Valentine cards and, around 1830, began importing lace and fine papers for her business, thus making her one of the first career women in the United States. The tradition of sending cards remained very popular until the Civil War, but the tradition died out until World War II when American soldiers stationed in the United Kingdom revived the custom on both sides of the Atlantic by sending love messages back home. Today the number of Valentine cards sent is second only to Christmas cards. And very often gifts and candy accompany the card. Not surprisingly, the greeting-card industry has claimed Saint Valentine as their patron.

SAINT PATRICK'S DAY—MARCH 17

On Saint Patrick's Day, it is traditional in America to wear green in honor of Saint Patrick, one of the patron saints of Ireland. The first Saint Patrick's Day celebration in the United States is said to have taken place in 1737 in Boston, where a number of Irish immigrants settled.

Observance of Saint Patrick's Day spread rapidly to other American cities, reaching the West Coast by the 1870s. Over 120,000 marchers have taken part in New York City's Saint Patrick's Day parade, which passes by Saint Patrick's Cathedral. In the Midwest, the Chicago River is spiked with green food coloring for the occasion. It is no wonder that on "Saint Paddy's Day" we hear lots of Irish music and see shamrocks, elves, harps, and pipes in store and school windows: There are more Irish in New York City alone than in all of Ireland.

The Irish are somewhat more restrained about celebrating Saint Patrick's Day than their kin in North America. Each local community usually has a parade with bands in full regalia. And many Irish Catholics take the day off from Lent to eat and drink their fill. Saint Patrick's Day also marks the end of cold weather and the start of the springtime planting of potatoes.

Wearing the green is also one of the traditions of Saint Patrick's Day in Ireland. According to legend, followers of Saint Patrick were put in a house made of dry wood, while the followers of a Protestant were put in a house made of green wood. Both houses were torched. The Protestants were burnt, but Saint Patrick's followers came out unharmed. So the green is worn to this day, perhaps as a form of protection.

WHAT OTHER SAINTS' FEAST DAYS ARE POPULAR?

SAINT DAVID'S DAY—MARCH 1
WALES

The patron saint of Wales is Saint David, a native Welshman whose father was a chieftain and an uncle of King Arthur. David was ordained a priest and spent several years in a monastery before emerging to persuade many Welsh to become Christians. He assured the bards of Wales that their musical talents would continue in the new religion. Many joined monastic orders, playing the harp, singing, and teaching in the monasteries, thereby ensuring that the musical tradition of Wales would survive to this day.

There is a legend that David once led an army to victory against the neighboring Saxons. On the way to battle, they passed through a field of leeks, whereupon David advised his soldiers to pull them up and wear them in their headgear to distinguish themselves from their enemies. The leek has long been a national emblem of Wales and is worn in hats on Saint David's Day.

Upon his death, Saint Kentigern at Llanelly reported that he saw Saint David's soul taken to heaven by angels. His body was later taken from the monastery church where he had lived such a quiet, austere life, to Saint David's Cathedral, where his tomb is still on view. Today, Saint

David's Day is celebrated by Welsh around the world with choral singing.

SAINT GEORGE'S DAY—APRIL 23
ENGLAND

> For thou, amongst those saints whom thou dost see,
> Shall be a saint and thine own country's friend
> And patron. Thou Saint George shall calléd be,
> Saint George of Merry England, the sign of Victory.
>
> —*Edmund Spenser*

Although Saint George is the patron saint of England, he never actually visited the fair isle. Nonetheless, his tales of dragon slaying, prowess, and daring captured the imagination of the English people.

Saint George was born in Cappadocia, Asia Minor, in the last half of the third century. It is said that when the Emperor Diocletian began his persecution of Christians in A.D. 303, Saint George proclaimed his faith and resigned his commission in the army. He was arrested, tortured, and finally beheaded.

By the eighth century, his fame had reached England. After declaring that Saint George had helped him win an important battle, Richard the Lion-Hearted vowed to make him the patron saint of England. In 1222, a holiday was proclaimed in his honor, and in 1344, Edward III founded the Brotherhood of the Knights of Saint George, officially replacing Saint Edward the Confessor, king of England from 1042 to 1066, as the patron saint of England.

Today, Saint George's red cross appears on the English flag, as well as on the flag of the United Kingdom, the Union

Jack, and serves as the insignia of the Church of England. The holiday is becoming more and more popular in England, with cards and greetings exchanged, and the English flag proudly flown. Recently, the queen received a petition requesting a greater celebration of the day, so that it can be given "the prominence it deserves." It is interesting to note that England's greatest literary figure, William Shakespeare, was born and died on Saint George's Day.

SAINT JOHN THE BAPTIST'S DAY—JUNE 24
CANADA

The patron saint of the province of Québec is Saint Jean Baptiste or Saint John the Baptist, and the day is a national holiday in the province. The French-speaking people of Québec gather together to celebrate their unique heritage and culture, displaying their provincial flag—the *fleur-de-lis*. More recently, the holiday has been a rallying day for the separatist movement in Québec, which calls for the secession of the province from Canada.

SAINT JOHN THE BAPTIST'S DAY—JUNE 24
MEXICO

On Saint John the Baptist's Day, Mexicans decorate wells and fountains with masses of flowers, candles, and paper novelties, for John the Baptist is the saint of waters in Mexico. Crowds of people bathe in streams or rivers, reveling in the coolness of the waters and the festive atmosphere. But when it rains on this day, the elders say that Saint John is weeping, and the festivities are more subdued.

SAINT JOHN THE BAPTIST'S DAY—JUNE 24
SAINT PETER'S DAY—JUNE 29
BRAZIL

For Brazilians, June 24 marks the beginning of a week-long celebration. Bonfires are lit, fireworks and balloons decorate the skies, and everyone attends a party with lots of singing and dancing. Palm-readers tell fortunes for the coming year. Of the many superstitions about this day, it is said if you look into the water and see your face, you will live another year.

After a week of joyous partying, the week culminates with Saint Peter's Day. In honor of the patron of shipwrights and fishermen, boats are royally decorated and assembled in the ports and fishing villages. In a mass display of color and pageantry, they sail along the rivers, accompanied by music and fireworks, to a shrine erected to Saint Peter. Here the boats are blessed by the local father and return home, their captains no doubt ready for a little shuteye after all the celebrations!

SAINT SWITHIN'S DAY—JULY 15
ENGLAND

Saint Swithin's Day, if thou dost rain,
For forty days it will remain
Saint Swithin's Day, if thou art fair,
For forty days, 'twill rain nae mair.

—*Scottish poem*

Just as a groundhog's shadow on Groundhog Day forecasts the coming of spring for North Americans, Britains believe that if it rains on Saint Swithin's Day, July 15, it will continue to rain for forty days.

In the ninth century, in return for helping King Egbert of Wessex against the Danes, Saint Swithin was made the Bishop of Winchester and the chief advisor to the throne. But for all his power, Saint Swithin remained a humble man. He requested that, upon his death, his body should be buried outside the cathedral, where the rain would fall on his grave.

Legend has it that some time after Saint Swithin's death, the present bishop attempted to move the saint's body into a shrine within the cathedral. But on July 15, a heavy rain began to fall and lasted for forty days, and the Bishop gave up on his plan. Two centuries later, Saint Swithin's body was moved to its final resting place within the cathedral, where he became England's most popular healing saint.

SAINT ANNE'S DAY—JULY 26
CANADA

July 26 is the feast day of one of the patron saints of Canada, Saint Anne, the mother of Mary. On this day, gypsies from both Canada and the United States celebrate Santana—Saint Anna—by making a pilgrimage to Sainte Anne de Beaupré in Québec. There they camp on church property, prepare a special feast, and pray to Saint Anne.

SAINT MARTIN OF TOURS'S DAY—NOVEMBER 11
FRANCE

November 11 was known throughout the Middles Ages as Martinalia, the feast day of Saint Martin of Tours, the patron saint of France who died in A.D. 401. This festival took the place of Vinalia, the vintage feast of ancient Rome, and also supplanted a similar Greek celebration in honor of

Dionysus, the god of wine. Perhaps this is the reason why innkeepers and dispensers of good food chose Saint Martin to be their patron! But Saint Martin's life reflects little feasting and merriment.

As a Roman soldier stationed in Amiens, Martin met an almost naked beggar. He took pity on the man, but as he had no money, he cut his own cloak in two and gave the beggar half. That night, a vision of Christ, dressed in the half cloak, appeared to Martin in a dream and commended him for his kindness. The torn cloak became a treasured relic, and the place it was kept was called a chapelle (from the French *chape*, meaning cape). The person guarding the cloak was called the chapelaine. From these words we get the English words *chapel* and *chaplain*.

Martin was given a piece of land by Saint Hilary to found a monastery, where he lived an ascetic life with a number of other hermits. Tradition has it that this was the first monastic community founded in Gaul, now known as France. A number of miracles were attributed to him and in A.D. 371, the people of Tours demanded him for their bishop. Many people in the area were converted to Christianity, and the miracles continued. After his death in A.D. 397, his cult became very popular, drawing many pilgrims to his burial site.

SAINT ANDREW'S DAY—NOVEMBER 30
SCOTLAND

Saint Andrew was born in Bethsaida, a town in Galilee. A fisherman by trade, along with his brother, Simon (later called Peter), he was the first of Jesus' disciples. Little is known of his subsequent travels, but legend says that he preached in Asia Minor, Macedonia, and Russia after Jesus' death. He is said to have been bound on an X-shaped cross in Patras in Achaia and continued to preach until he died two days later. In the fourth century a certain Saint Rule had charge of the relics of Saint Andrew and was warned by an angel to take them to a place that would be indicated. He traveled in a northwesterly direction until he was stopped by a sign from the angel at a place we now know as Saint Andrews, Scotland. Here he built a church to shelter the relics and was eventually made its first bishop.

Some Scots wear blue and white ribbons shaped like an X on the feast of Saint Andrew. The blue and white cross is also on the flag of Scotland.

Saint Nicholas of Myra's Day—December 6
Netherlands/Holland

In the Netherlands, it is common practice to give children gifts on the feast day of Saint Nicholas, the patron saint of Amsterdam. The tradition of Santa Claus came to North America with Dutch Protestants, who settled in what was then called New Amsterdam—later known as New York. They brought with them their traditions of gift-giving on December 6, the feast of Saint Nicholas. In the New World these traditions mixed with Scandinavian legends about a wizard who rewarded good children with presents. During the Victorian era, the gift-giving custom spread rapidly around the world, spurred on by the first Christmas cards.

In Holland today, children who leave empty clogs out on the eve of Sinter Klaes find them filled with candies and small gifts the next day! Presents that arrive on December 25 are said to be brought by the Christ Child.

Day of Our Lady of Guadalupe—December 12
Mexico

December 12 is the day of Mexico's greatest festival, which celebrates the appearance of the Virgin Mary to a Mexican peasant by the name of Juan Diego in December 1531. It happened at the spot where the Spanish had destroyed the ancient Aztec shrine to Tonantzin, their goddess of the earth and growing corn. The Virgin Mary requested that Juan Diego go to the bishop with the message that a church be built for her on that spot.

When the bishop didn't believe him, Mary appeared to Juan Diego again, filling his blanket with Castilian roses (which are foreign to Mexico) and telling him to return once again to the bishop. When the roses tumbled out of the blanket and a portrait of Mary appeared on it, the bishop was convinced and a church was built. It is reported that this blanket with Mary's portrait hangs today in the church just outside of Mexico City and is in pristine condition.

Each year, this story is enacted in a puppet show witnessed by thousands of pilgrims. Special offerings of roses, pigs, chickens, and eggs are made, and altars are decorated with flickering candles. Images of the Virgin are placed on patios and in windows of the faithful, making the streets festive. After Lourdes in France and Fátima in Portugal, this is considered to be one of the world's greatest pilgrimages.

Saint Lucy's Day—December 13
Sweden

In Sweden, as well as a number of other Scandinavian countries, Yuletide starts on Luciadagen, Saint Lucy's Day. All the preparation for Christmas must be done; the house cleaned, the baking completed, the gifts bought. The holiday fish, the cutfish, is placed in beech ashes and buried, ready for dinner on Christmas Eve.

Saint Lucy was born of noble parents in Syracuse, Sicily. While she was still young, she offered her virginity to God, but kept the vow a secret. When her mother later pressed her to marry a young pagan, Lucy persuaded her to pray at the tomb of Saint Agatha for relief from a hemorrhage. When her mother was miraculously healed, Saint Lucy revealed her desire to give herself to God and her fortune to the poor. Her mother agreed, but her suitor revealed Lucy as a Christian, and she was put to death in A.D. 304.

To represent Saint Lucy, a young girl dressed in a long white gown with a crimson sash and a crown of leaves carrying lighted white candles goes to neighboring homes early in the morning with a tray of cakes and coffee. She is often accompanied by local boys and girls who sing carols. The boys are called Star Boys, for they are also dressed all in white with pointed silver caps. They must be a welcome sight on a cold, dark winter morning.

WHAT IS ALL SAINTS' DAY?

In many ways, All Saints' Day—or All Hallows, as it was often called in England—is a catchall for the many feast days that are missed throughout the year. There are so many saints, it's impossible to celebrate each one. In A.D. 609, Pope Boniface IV converted the ancient Roman Pantheon, which was erected in honor of all the Roman gods, into a place of Christian worship consecrated to the Virgin Mary and all the martyrs. A century later, Pope Gregory II dedicated a chapel in Saint Peter's Cathedral in Rome to all the saints, establishing November 1 as their festival.

The evening of the day before is known as All Saints' Eve, or All Hallows' Eve, "The night between the Saints and the Souls/When the bodiless gang aboot." In parts of England it was the custom to take bundles of straw to a hilltop, set fire to them, and toss them in the air. These were the "holy souls" escaping from purgatory to heaven. Children in North America now celebrate this night by trick-or-treating.

WHAT IS MICHAELMAS DAY?

Michaelmas Day, September 29, was originally celebrated in honor of Saint Michael the Archangel and all angels. Today, by order of the Vatican, the feast also honors Saint Gabriel and Saint Raphael.

Michaelmas Day was so popular over the years that the profusely blooming flower of early autumn was named the Michaelmas daisy. The other festival for Saint Michael, May 8, commemorated his appearance (September 29 was the date of the dedication of his basilica on the Salarian Way near Rome). Michael is often shown in armor with a flaming sword and one foot on the fallen Satan. To early Christians, he was the protector of the sick, and many hot springs were dedicated to him. Cliffs also came under his care as the guardian of mountains. As a result, many churches and convents were built on cliffs, the most famous being Mont-Saint-Michel on the northwestern coast of France. Saint

Michael is also the patron saint of Germany, grocers, paratroopers, police, and radiologists.

Saint Raphael's feast day was October 24. His name means "God has healed," and this, coupled with stories of healings by him, has caused Raphael to be identified as the angel who moved the healing waters by the Sheep Gate in biblical times. People would lie by this pool, waiting for the waters to "be troubled," so that they could step into the spring for healing (John 5:1-9). Raphael is the patron saint of the blind, nurses, physicians, and travelers.

Gabriel is the angel who announced to Mary that she would bear the Son of God. So perhaps it was fitting that his feast day, March 24, was the day before the feast of the Annunciation of the Blessed Virgin. And appropriately so, Saint Gabriel is the patron saint of broadcasters, clerics, messengers, postal employees, radio workers, telecommunications workers, telephone workers, and television workers.

WHAT IS SAINT URHO'S DAY?

In Thunder Bay, Ontario, Canada, Saint Patrick's Day festivities are "crashed" every year by Finns celebrating the feast day of Saint Urho, Finland's patron saint. Thunder Bay has the largest Finnish population outside of Finland. These Canadian Finns feel that the Saint Patrick's Day festivities overshadow those of Saint Urho's feast day, which falls on March 16. As Saint Urho is credited with saving the grape arbors of Finland from a terrible plague of grasshoppers, celebrants of his feast day drink grape juice and march around in blue-green and purple costumes chanting, "Grasshopper, grasshopper, go away." Apparently no one minds—not even the Saint Patrick's Day revelers, who usually offer to buy Saint Urho's celebrants a drink!

HOW IS SAINT ANTHONY'S DAY CELEBRATED?

Credited with curing beasts of the plague during the Middle Ages, Saint Anthony is the patron saint of herdsmen and domestic animals. Originally, his feast day of January 17 was celebrated with a blessing of the animals. The first celebration of the blessing of the animals took place in Rome in the nineteenth century. Over the centuries, the celebration spread to the New World, where it has become most popular in Latin America.

Today, the blessing of animals is celebrated in Los Angeles with a parade of pets—although nowadays not on Saint Anthony's feast day itself but on Holy Saturday, the day before Easter. It rained so often on Saint Anthony's feast day that the parade was moved to springtime! Pets and their owners gather in the morning on Olvera Street. The animals are gaily decorated with ribbons and flowers and then paraded along Sunset Boulevard to the church. At the church, a priest sprinkles each animal with holy water, as he prays:

> Almighty Father, we bless the animals for all they have done for us in supplying our food, carrying our burdens, and providing companionship, and rendering a service to mankind since the world began.

After the priest prays for the animals' health, well-being, and fertility, white doves are released, and Mexican musicians play while the animals parade back to Olvera Street—for a special treat!

DO WE CELEBRATE ANY OTHER DAYS FOR ANIMALS?

The World Day for Animals occurs every October 4 on the feast day of Saint Francis of Assisi, who is the patron saint of animal welfare societies. At the Church of Saint John the Baptist in New York, children and adults bring their pets to church on this day to be blessed. Reportedly, the largest animal ever to attend was an elephant!

HOW DID THE TRADITION OF HOT CROSS BUNS BEGIN?

There are many legends of how the tradition of serving hot cross buns during Lent began, but perhaps one of the most interesting concerns the daughter of an Assisi nobleman, known to us today as Saint Clare. Clare wanted very much to be a teacher of the Christian faith, but when her parents disapproved, she fled to a small chapel where Saint Francis was preaching. Here she laid her fine clothes before the altar. Saint Francis gave her his habit of sackcloth to wear and cut off her hair. Although her family and friends tried to convince her to leave the convent, she remained steadfast in her resolve. Saint Francis later appointed her the first abbess of a convent just outside of Assisi.

One day the pope came for a visit and asked Saint Clare to bless the small buns they were about to eat. Reportedly, as soon as she made the sign of the cross, the cross appeared on each one of the buns!

Hot cross buns became very popular in England, where they were sold by street vendors for breakfast on Good Friday. Some people would hang a bun in their homes, replacing it each Good Friday, believing it would ward off evil spirits and safeguard their homes. The English brought the custom with them to the New World, where the tasty little treats eventually became so popular that we now can find them in food stores throughout Lent.

ARE THERE ANY SAINTS' FEAST DAYS ON CHRISTMAS DAY?

In addition to the principal feast of the birthday of Jesus, another minor feast occurs on December 25. Saint Anastasia is commemorated in the second Mass of Christmas Day in the Roman Catholic Church. She was the daughter of a noble Roman who married a pagan named Publius. After his death, Anastasia went to Aquileia to help the Christians there and was arrested and imprisoned. A vision of Saint Theodota visited her in prison, and when Anastasia was put aboard a vessel and abandoned at sea, Saint Theodota appeared again to pilot the ship safely back to land. All on board were converted to Christianity. However, the authorities caught up with Anastasia, and she was eventually taken to the island of Palmaria and burned alive.

WHAT CHRISTMAS TRADITIONS ARE LINKED TO SAINTS?

CHRISTMAS TREE

What would Christmas be like without a Christmas tree? Well, if it hadn't been for Saint Boniface, Christmas would look very different. Saint Boniface was born in Devonshire, England, in A.D. 680. After becoming an ordained priest, he obtained permission from the pope to preach to the Germanic tribes. According to legend, Saint Boniface encouraged them to forsake their pagan rites in the forests, which were centered around the sacred oak tree. Instead, he urged them to carry small fir trees into their homes and decorate them at Yuletide, the ancient feast of the winter solstice, which came to be celebrated with the Christian festival of Christ's birth.

Later, Martin Luther is said to have lighted a tree with candles, a tradition that continues in many European countries and is the forerunner of the electrical lights often seen on Christmas trees today.

GIFT-GIVING

The legend of Saint Nicholas is widely believed to be linked to the tradition of gift-giving on Christmas Eve.

Nicholas was born to aristocrats in Asia Minor and later became a bishop. When he inherited his parents' money, he generously gave it to the poor and those in need. On one occasion, a poor neighbor of Nicholas was on the verge of selling his three daughters into slavery because he did not have money for dowries to marry them off properly. One night, Nicholas tossed three bags full of gold through a window into the neighbor's house, saving the daughters from lives of servitude. From these first gifts, we can trace the Dutch tradition of giving gifts on the eve of Saint Nicholas's feast day, December 6. And in America and much of Europe, the tradition has shifted to coincide with a visit from jolly old Saint Nick on the eve of the birth of Jesus.

CRÈCHE

We have Saint Francis of Assisi to thank for all the nativity scenes, or crèches, that we see on people's lawns and in the churches. In 1223 at Greccio, Italy, Saint Francis set up the first nativity scene—using real people and live animals. He told his friend John Da Vellita, "I would make a memorial of that Child who was born in Bethlehem and in some sort behold with bodily eyes the hardships of his infant state, lying on hay in a manger with the ox and the ass standing by."[15] That Christmas, the local peasants flocked to the midnight mass held at the hermitage to hear Saint Francis speak on the mystery of the Christmas message.

Saint Francis's great love for animals also sparked the tradition of giving working animals a rest and some extra rations on Christmas Eve. During Dickens's time, horses were often given a drink of ale or a piece of Christmas pudding just to ensure good health.

DO WE CELEBRATE ANY SAINTS' BIRTHDAYS?

Saint John the Baptist's birthday (June 24) is celebrated as his feast day instead of the day of his death. (The birthdays of the Virgin Mary and Jesus are also celebrated.) The feast of Saint John the Baptist took the place of the pagan festival of Baal, the sun god, during the summer solstice or midsummer. Today, in the Eastern Church, his festival is second only to the one held for the Virgin Mary.

CHAPTER NINE

WHO ARE THE MOST FAMOUS SAINTS?

Lord, make me an instrument of your peace.
Where there is hatred, let me sow love,
Where there is injury, pardon,
Where there is doubt, faith,
Where there is despair, hope,
Where there is darkness, light,
Where there is sadness, joy.

O Divine Master, grant that I may not so much seek
to be consoled as to console,
not so much to be understood as to understand,
not so much to be loved, as to love;
for it is in giving that we receive,
it is in pardoning that we are pardoned,
it is in dying, that we awake to eternal life. AMEN.

—attributed to Saint Francis of Assisi
(12th century)

There are many famous saints—but those whose popularity endures the passing centuries tend to be those who lived ordinary lives. From what we know about them, they were people, like you and me, who never knew Jesus personally. So you will not find the popular archangels, Michael, Gabriel, or Raphael, nor the Apostles, nor Jesus' friends and relatives in this listing of famous saints. Nevertheless, the saints described here displayed a great love for their God and for others. They are the better part of all of us.

SAINT FRANCIS OF ASSISI
FEAST DAY—OCTOBER 4
Patronage: Italy, Catholic Action, animals, merchants, ecologists

Saint Francis of Assisi is probably the most beloved of all the saints. He was born at Assisi in Umbria, Italy, in 1181 and christened Giovanni. Some say his name was later changed to Francis, meaning the Frenchman, because of his fondness for France. Francis decided early in his adult life to devote himself to the care of the poor and sick. According to tradition, Francis heard the voice of Jesus directing him to rebuild His church while he was at prayer. Francis took this literally and took money from his father's fortune to upgrade the local church.

His father disowned the young man, and Francis began his religious life living in a small hut. People were drawn to his simple life, and the Franciscan order was founded. It was in his honor that Franciscan friars, doing missionary work in the New World, named the Bay of San Francisco. Saint Francis is probably best known to us today for his great love for all living things. He could talk with the animals, and communicate with the skies. His gentleness and pleasant disposition attract people today as much as seven hundred years ago.

SAINT NICHOLAS OF BARI, BISHOP OF MYRA
FEAST DAY—DECEMBER 6
Patronage: children, Greece, Russia, bakers, brides, pawnbrokers, prisoners, sailors, apothecaries, merchants, perfumers

Is there a saint better known today than Saint Nicholas? Due to the association we have with him and Santa Claus, he's probably the most popular modern-day figure—at least with children! We know little about the man other than legend. It is said that his parents knew he was destined for sainthood from his early years, when he would refuse to nurse on fasting days and would stand on his little legs praising God.

His patronage for small children comes not from the giving of gifts but from the story that he raised three boys from the dead. It is said that Nicholas was staying at the inn where the children had been kidnapped and killed during a local food shortage. The innkeeper intended to use them as food for the guests. But when Nicholas came to the inn for a meal, he immediately sensed what was going on. He went down to the basement of the inn and resurrected the boys.

Tales of miracles and kindness abound about Nicholas. He continues to be one of the most widely venerated saints, and his spirit of giving is certainly the essence of the Christmas season.

SAINT PATRICK
FEAST DAY—MARCH 17
Patronage: Ireland

Saint Patrick's feast day is one of the most celebrated worldwide. But legend has it that this patron saint of Ireland was British by birth, carried off by marauding pirates and sold into slavery to an Irish master. Here he spent six harsh years of his life, vowing to one day dedicate his life to God. He finally escaped from his master's farm, and fled to Britain where he was reunited with his family. Eventually he went on to France and later became a bishop of the Church. But his visions kept telling him to return to Ireland, so when Saint Palladius, the missionary bishop to Ireland, died, Saint Patrick rejoiced when he was sent to replace him.

For the remaining years of his life, Patrick worked to convert the Irish. His miraculous feats were numerous—he is credited with driving all the snakes out of Ireland and spontaneously lighting an Easter fire on the hillside at Slane. It is said that he explained the concept of the Trinity to the people by using the shamrock, the emblem which remains his to this day.

SAINT VALENTINE
FEAST DAY—FEBRUARY 14
Patronage: lovers

Oddly enough, the martyrdom of two saints named Valentine is celebrated on February 14! We know very little about these saints, who are commonly thought of as being one person.

As you may have already read, our tradition of picking a valentine comes from the Roman festival of Lupercalia. There was also a popular English belief, recorded in literature around the time of Chaucer, that the birds would begin to mate around February 14, prompting thoughts of love in young men and women.

SAINT CHRISTOPHER
FEAST DAY—JULY 25
Patronage: motorists, porters, sailors, travelers

The cult of Saint Christopher was extremely popular during the Middle Ages and was revived in this century due to his new patronage of travelers and motorists. It's hard to find his medallion, though, for the Roman Catholic Church reduced his cult to local veneration in 1969 due to the lack of hard evidence that he actually lived. But Christopher, the massive man who ferried the Christ child on his back across the raging river, will likely remain for a while in the public's favor; it is hard to resist the thought of having a kindly giant for protection when traveling on vacation!

SAINT GEORGE
FEAST DAY—APRIL 23
Patronage: England, Portugal, Germany, Greece, Boy Scouts, armorers, butchers, saddlers, soldiers, archers, knights (specifically, the Order of the Garter), and husbands as the protectors of women

As a model "white knight in shining armor," Saint George is the ultimate hero of chivalry and was very popular during the fourteenth and fifteenth centuries. Here's the famous story of George slaying the dragon:

> There once was a terrible dragon who was killing anyone who got close enough to him. To appease the dragon, the citizens gave him two sheep a day, but

when all the sheep were gone, a human victim had to be found. A lottery was established, and the king's lovely daughter, Cleolinda, drew a losing ticket. She nobly went to meet her fate and was tied up at the mouth of the dragon's cave. However, as luck would have it, she had met George on the way, and he had promised to save her through the power of his Lord, Jesus Christ. When the dragon appeared, he speared it with his lance, and, lassoing it with the princess' girdle, led it back to town. George offered to kill the dragon if the town would convert to Christianity. When they agreed, the dragon was slain, and 15,000 people were baptized. George refused any reward, asking that it instead be given to the poor, and he rode away.

As the protector of England, George's popularity is on the rise today in that country. But the Roman Catholic Church decided to reduce his status to local veneration in 1969 (like Saint Christopher, because of a lack of evidence that he actually lived), so that his feast day is no longer observed by the Church worldwide.

SAINT JOAN OF ARC
FEAST DAY—MAY 30
Patronage: France, soldiers

Jeanne la Pucelle (better known as Joan of Arc) was born in 1412 in the region of Champagne, France, to a young peasant farmer and his gentle wife. As a young girl, Joan witnessed the invasion of Normandy by Henry V of England and the overthrow of the French king, Charles VI. When she was fourteen years old, she began to hear the voices of Saint Catherine of Alexandria, Margaret of Antioch, and Michael, the archangel, which revealed her mission to save

France. She finally took her message to the Dauphin, the eldest son of the king of France, and convinced him to listen to her. At her instruction, troops led by Joan herself were sent to Orleans, and a great victory resulted. The Dauphin was crowned King Charles VII with Joan by his side.

But Joan had disturbed the men at Charles's court, and soon she found herself kidnapped by the Duke of Burgundy and sold to the English. She was sent to an ecclesiastical tribunal at Rouen, where she was questioned day and night. Finally, she admitted to hearing voices, and she was told to stop wearing men's armor. Joan soon disregarded this admonition, was recaptured, declared to be a lapsed heretic, and burned at the stake. She had not yet reached her twentieth birthday. Four hundred and fifty years later on May 16, 1920, she was solemnly canonized. In France today, the *Fête de Jeanne D'Arc* is celebrated on the second Sunday in May.

SAINT VINCENT DE PAUL
FEAST DAY—JULY 19
Patronage: charitable groups

Throughout North America, the name Saint Vincent de Paul is synonymous with the word *charity*. Born in Gascony, France, in 1580, Vincent became an ordained priest when he was only twenty years old. He was drawn to help the underprivileged, working with the galley slaves in Paris, and in 1622, was given a mission to the convict slaves at Bordeaux. With the help of his new order, the Lazarists or Vincentians, he founded colleges and missions around the world and hospitals for the sick, aged, and orphans. Along with Saint Louise de Marillac, he established charities to aid the poor and sick in each parish. From this sprang the Sisters of Charity, and Vincent managed to bring together the wealthy women of Paris to collect funds or do good deeds.

During his lifetime, missions were sent to the poor in Poland, Ireland, and Scotland, among other places, and over 1,200 slaves were ransomed in North Africa. It is not surprising that so much work took a toll on his health. He suffered much from illness in his later years, dying peacefully in his chair. In 1833, Frederic Ozanam founded the Saint Vincent de Paul Society in Paris. The spirit of good deeds that inspires its members is the heart and soul of the great man after whom it is named.

Saint Catherine of Alexandria
Feast day—November 25
Patronage: maidens, philosophers, preachers, nurses, students, the dying, wheelwrights, spinners, potters, millers

History tells us nothing of Catherine of Alexandria, who lived in the fourth century, yet she was one of the most popular saints of the Middle Ages. Legend says that she was born the daughter of a pagan princess in Egypt, with a halo already circling her head. She spent a quiet childhood, meditating and studying. When her father died, Catherine was made queen at the age of fourteen, and numerous suitors offered to marry her, all of whom she declined. When a hermit showed her a likeness of the Virgin Mary and Jesus, Catherine was instantly converted and zealously began to protest the persecution of Christians by the Roman emperor Maxentius.

Maxentius fell in love with the beautiful queen and attempted to seduce her. When all attempts failed, he sent fifty philosophers to straighten Catherine out. She converted all of them. Maxentius then threw her in prison, but she converted not only her guards but also the empress! When nothing could persuade the girl to fall for his advances, Maxentius ordered her to be killed on a spiked wheel. Just as she was being placed between the teeth of the wheel, it was struck by lightning, shattering the wheel and injuring many onlookers. (From this event we get our Catherine-wheel fireworks.) Finally, the emperor ordered Catherine to be beheaded. A white, milk-like liquid flowed from her veins.

Today, Catherine's cult has been totally suppressed by the Roman Catholic Church. But her supporters on Mt. Sinai, where her relics were carried by angels, remain strong in their veneration of this popular saint.

SAINT FRANCIS XAVIER
FEAST DAY—DECEMBER 3
Patronage: East Indies, Japan, Australia, New Zealand, foreign missions

Born in 1506 at the castle of Xavier in Spanish Navarre, Francis went to study at the University of Paris when he was eighteen. There he met Ignatius of Loyola and became one of the first Jesuits who offered themselves to the service of God at Montmartre in 1534. Six years later, Ignatius appointed him the first missionary to the East Indies.

After a harsh sea voyage of thirteen months (nearly twice the usual time), his first stop was at Goa, where the local Christians were beating their slaves and counting the blows on their rosaries. Francis reformed the Christians and set up his mission, visiting the sick and the poor. He set the basics of the Christian religion to the tune of popular songs, which the local people could sing everywhere they went.

In his travels, Francis had heard of the Japanese islands, where no missionary had been before. He was determined to go, and arrived finally in April 1549 at Kagoshima on Kyushu. There he soon realized that impoverished dress did not impress the Japanese, so he decided to present himself in a more dignified manner. He baptized many throughout the islands of Japan.

Next, he set his sights on China, a country closed to foreign visitors. But before he could arrange transportation, an illness struck him and he died in the early morning of December 3, 1552. His body was packed in lime just in case it needed to be moved in the future. More than ten weeks later, the coffin was opened. Francis Xavier's body showed no decomposition. It was taken back to Goa, where its continued incorruption was verified by physicians, and it was enshrined in the Church of the Good Jesus. There it can be visited today. Saint Francis Xavier was canonized in 1622 along with Saints Ignatius of Loyola, Teresa of Avila, Philip Neri, and Isidore the Husbandman.

IS JESUS A SAINT?

Jesus is the son of God, part of the Holy Trinity, and is thus set apart from the ranks of the saints. The Roman Catholic Church celebrates many Feasts of Our Lord, which are days when the worship of God has a special reference to an event in the earthly life of Jesus.

His Circumcision	January 1
His Holy Name	January 2
The Epiphany	January 6
Easter	Springtime

His Ascension	40th day after Easter
Finding of the Cross	May 3
His Precious Blood	July 1
His Sacred Heart,	
His Transfiguration	August 6
Corpus Christi, the	
Exaltation of the Cross	September 14
Christ the King	last Sunday in October
Dedication of the Basilica of Saint Saviour	November 9
His Birthday	December 25

WHICH SAINTS ARE MOST COMMONLY FOUND IN POPULAR CULTURE?

No doubt the most common saint in Western pop culture is good old Saint Nick. But a number of other saints have also made their way into the pop culture of today: Saint Christopher is a favorite among cabbies, especially in New York City, and has been immortalized in song by Tom Waits. The Grateful Dead also sing of Saint Stephen. Saint Elmo has a movie named after him, *Saint Elmo's Fire*, and a Saint Bernard dog is often visible in TV commercials and has the starring role in the movie *Beethoven*.

"When the Saints Go Marching In" is a popular spiritual song today, just as it was years ago. It is often played in New Orleans at funeral processions as part of the lively music after the service is over. It is likely that the saints referred to were the members of the Sanctified church, which arose with the Holiness movement of the late nineteenth century in the southern United States. Those who were said to be chosen by the Holy Ghost could go into a trance, speak in tongues, or break into a "holy dance," any of which was proof positive of their initiation into the congregation of saints.

A verse from the Reverend Rice's song, "Testify—For My Lord is Coming Back Again" goes like this (unfortunately without the brass, bass, piano, and tambourine):

> Sanctified father, sanctified son,
> Sanctified people, all are one
> If you're not sanctified — can't go in —
> For my Lord is Coming Back again.[16]

WHO ARE THE SAINTS IN THE CHURCH OF JESUS CHRIST OF LATTER-DAY SAINTS?

According to Heber C. Kimball, one of the early Mormon international missionaries, "Those who believed in Paul's testimony were saints of God; those who believed Joseph Smith's are just as surely saints, for it is the same gospel."[17]

Just as Saint Paul stated that all followers of Christ are saints, Joseph Smith preached likewise: All who followed his doctrine were saints as well. Mormons refer to all non-Mormons, except for Jews, as Gentiles. It is interesting that the Church of Jesus Christ of Latter-Day Saints is one of the fastest-growing denominations in the world today. At the time of founder Joseph Smith's death in 1844, the Latter-Day Saints numbered forty thousand. By 1877, the year of Brigham Young's death, that number rose to one hundred fifty thousand. The one million mark was reached in 1947, and five million in 1982. Statistics like these make the question "How many saints are there?" difficult to answer!

WHAT IS SAINT ELMO'S FIRE?

The "fire" is the bluish electrical discharge that emanates from charged, usually pointed objects, such as the tips of ships' masts or church spires. This electrical glow can often be seen before and after a storm. In medieval times, sailors anxiously looked for this "fire" to show that their ship had been taken under the protection of their patron saint, Elmo. Legend has it that Saint Elmo, also known as Erasmus, once preached a complete sermon in the middle of a terrible thunderstorm, undeterred by the bolts of lightning that struck the ground all around him.

WHAT IS SAINT MARTIN'S SUMMER?

Whereas North Americans have Indian summer, the English and the French refer to their pleasant respite before oncoming winter weather as Saint Martin's summer. Because Saint Martin of Tours's feast day of November 11 occurs around the time of this last wave of summer weather, his name has been lent to this season. William Shakespeare refers to this in *Henry VI*, when Joan of Arc says:

> Assign'd am I to be the English scourge.
> This night the seige assuredly I'll raise;
> Expect Saint Martin's summer, halcyon days,
> Since I have entered into these wars.

> *(1.2.129-132)*

WHY DID COBBLERS CALL MONDAY, SAINT MONDAY?

Here's a case where merrymakers might have gone a bit too far. In the Middle Ages, tradespeople often took the day off to celebrate their profession's patron saint's feast day. Well, it seems that cobblers seldom worked on Mondays, and because every Monday was a "holiday" for them, they didn't know which Monday was the feast day of their patron saint, Saint Crispin or Crispian. So, in order to not miss Saint Crispin's feast day, they decided to celebrate *every* Monday!

After the Battle of Agincourt, which was fought and won by the English on the feast of Saint Crispin (October 25), the day became very popular in England. For example, in Shakespeare's *Henry V*, the king says to his soldiers:

> This day is called the feast of Crispian.
> He who outlives this day and comes safe home

Shall stand a-tiptoe when this is named
And rouse him at the name of Crispian.

(4.3.40-43)

HOW DID THE SAINT BERNARD DOG GET ITS NAME?

Saint Bernard of Montjoux (A.D. 996–1081) was responsible for the safety of travelers, many of whom were on pilgrimage to Rome, through the passes. Bernard managed to rid the passes of robbers and established hospices where travelers could stay.

Saint Bernard dogs were originally kept by the Augustine monks of the Little and Great Saint Bernard Passes in the Swiss Alps. The monks named the breed after Saint Bernard of Montjoux. The dogs were specially trained to rescue travelers who had become lost in the snow in the treacherous passes, which were also named after the saint.

WHAT IS SAINT ANTHONY'S FIRE?

If you have Saint Anthony's fire, you would surely want to invoke Saint Anthony to help cure it. The "fire" is a red, sometimes very painful inflammation of the skin caused by ergotism (a contagious disease caused by eating grains of rye or wheat that have been damaged with a fungus called ergo). In the eleventh century, the Order of the Hospitallers of Saint Anthony was founded to care for people suffering from the disease.

WHAT IS SAINT VITUS'S DANCE?

Saint Vitus's dance is better known to us today as chorea, a disorder of the nervous system that produces irregular, jerking movements caused by the muscles contracting involuntarily. Saint Vitus is invoked by people suffering from this disease, as well as those who have epileptic seizures. The body movements caused by chorea sometimes resembled those of a dancer, hence the name, Saint Vitus's dance, and his patronage of dancers.

WHAT ARE SAINT JOHN'S FIRES?

The feast of Saint John the Baptist takes place on June 24, the same day as the ancient festival of Baal, the pagan sun god. Long ago, bonefires (hence, bonfires) were lit during this festival to consume the animal sacrifices to the sun. The practice continued after Christianity came to Britain, but animals were no longer involved. These ritual fires came to be called Saint John's fires, as the pagan holiday merged with Saint John's feast day.

WHAT IS SAINT-JOHN'S-WORT?

Saint-John's-wort (*Hypericum perforatum*) is a medicinal herb. Its yellow flowers and leaves contain oil and pigment-filled glands that are blood-red when held to the light. It was believed that the curative properties of the plant were more potent if the flowers were picked as they were just opening, around Saint John the Baptist's Day on June 24. The flowers were burned along with other sacred herbs in bonfires, purifying the air to protect people, livestock, and crops. The oil produced from the flowers, called Saint John's oil, has been used for centuries. According to the Swiss herbalist Father Künzle: "It heals quickly all stings, cuts, and abrasions and should therefore be kept in every household."

WHAT IS SAINT JOSEPH'S OIL?

In early Christianity, oil was a common medicinal remedy (James 5:14-15):

> Is any among you sick? Let him call for the elders of the church, and let them pray over him, anointing him with oil in the name of the Lord; and the prayer of faith

will save the sick man, and the Lord will raise him up; and if he has committed sins, he will be forgiven.

The Brothers of the Holy Cross, a group of French teachers who were very devoted to Saint Joseph, always wore medals picturing the saint instead of crucifixes. When they came to North America, they brought with them the local folk custom of anointing the sick with oil that had burned before the image of Saint Joseph and rubbing them with a medal of the saint.

This custom is still being practiced. During the first part of this century, Blessed Brother André used Saint Joseph's oil when healing the sick.

WHAT ARE THE HOLY VERONICA?

Saint Veronica, whose feast day is July 12, is the subject of one of the most beloved legends in Christendom. It is said that the image of the face of Jesus was imprinted on her veil, after she tenderly wiped away the blood from His face as He made His Way to the Cross. The original cloth is claimed to be among the highly treasured relics of Saint Peter's in Rome. Did this really happen? While we can acknowledge the love expressed by the action of the woman who comforted Jesus, the accuracy of her name, Veronica, has been the subject of much speculation. In early Christianity, true images of Jesus were called *vera icon*. Subsequently these images came to be called veronica—hence, the name of the woman on the Way to the Cross.

WHAT IS SAINT ALL FOOLS' DAY?

April 1st, commonly known as April Fools' Day, is the feast day of Saint Hugh, Bishop of Grenoble. But we get April Fools' Day from a different source. In 1582, the Gregorian calendar (the one we follow today) was adopted, moving New Year's Day from March 25 to January 1. People who forgot the change continued to make their traditional New Year's visits just after the old March date and were mocked by their friends as "Saint All-Fool." Gradually, the custom changed and tricks were played on unsuspecting victims on the first day in April.

WHAT IS SAINT BENEDICT'S HERB?

Legend has it that Saint Benedict gave his blessing to this medicinal herb (*Geum urbanum*), for it was said to eliminate all foreign elements from the eyes, nose, teeth, brain, and heart. In the Swiss Alps, shepherds tie a bunch of the roots of this plant around the necks of their animals to cure inflammation of the eyes caused by cold winds.

WHAT ARE SAINT MARY'S GARDENS?

Numerous gardens were dedicated to the Virgin Mary in the Middle Ages. They were most often walled and full of beautiful, fragrant flowers and songbirds. Roses, symbolizing pure love and martyrdom, were popular in such gardens, as were lilies, signifying purity and innocence. Many names of flowers contained the words "Our Lady," although today the "Our" is often dropped. "Our Lady's mantle" and "Our Lady's smock," for example, have become simply "lady's mantle" and "lady's-smock." Here's a list of some flowers that can be found in a Saint Mary's garden:

> Mary's eyes (forget-me-nots)
> Marygolds (marigolds)
> Our Lady's keys (cowslip)
> Our Lady's thimble (harebell)
> Our Lady's tears (lily of the valley)

Legends about flowers with Marian connections are rife. The rose of Mary or rosemary's flowers are said to have changed from white to blue when Mary laid her blue cloak over the plant. And the white leaf veins of the blessed milk thistle are said to have come from Mary's milk.

WHO WAS SAINT TAMMANY?

During the Revolutionary War, American troops were amused by the British soldiers' strong belief that Saint George, patron saint of England, helped them in battle. So some American soldiers decided to adopt their own "patron saint." They chose, however, a rather disreputable seventeenth-century Delaware Indian chief named Tammanend. They called him Saint Tammany and declared May 12 as his feast day. The day was celebrated in ridiculous proportions, mocking the pomp and ceremony of the British troops.

After the Revolutionary War, the Society of Saint Tammany was formed, taking the name of the American troops' assumed saint. The name Tammany had come to represent patriotism and middle-class opposition to the power of the aristocratic Federalist Party. By the early nineteenth century, the Society's platform had become associated with that of the Democratic party and its meeting place became known as Tammany Hall. Unfortunately, the Society of Saint Tammany's record of bribing political leaders—among them the notorious "Boss" Tweed of New York City—has made the name Tammany synonymous with political corruption.

WHO ARE THE FROST SAINTS?

The Frost Saints are Saint Mamertus, Saint Pancras, and Saint Servatas. Their feast days fall one after the other on May 11, 12, and 13. In the wine-growing areas of Germany and France, frost can strike a costly blow at this time of year. German farmers call the Frost Saints the three severe lords and believe that crops are not safe until these days have passed. French peasants believe that frost is the result of offending one of these three saints. Some French peasants have even been known to flog the statues of the saints to show their displeasure at the cold weather!

WHO ARE THE PILLAR SAINTS?

Three pillar saints are listed in the *Roman Martyrology*, the elder and younger Simeone, and Daniel, a follower of Simeone the elder. In a rather bizarre spate of religious fanaticism, Saint Simeone Stylite (390–459 A.D.) decided to live on top of a six-foot-high column. He soon became so ashamed of his lack of courage (it was so low!), that he built column after column until one reached 60 feet high. Here he lived, with his disciples hoisting up his food in buckets and hauling away his waste. When he died, it is said that several days passed before anyone was aware of his death. Other Stylites, following his example to a degree, practiced a hermitic life not quite so extreme—the pillars were often not more than a few feet high, with a tiny hut on a platform, or a column-shaped cell where the holy man lived.

WHY DO PEOPLE THANK SAINTS, SUCH AS SAINT JUDE, IN THE NEWSPAPER?

There are often little notices in the newspapers that address certain saints. For example:

> Special Thanks to God, Saint Anthony, Saint Gerard, and Saint Benedict for favors received.

In such notices, petitioners are not only giving thanks publicly to a saint for favors received, they are also making other people aware of the saint's ability to help. Many petitioners believe that one way of making the favor binding is to print a formal thank-you in the newspaper.

WHAT IS SAINT PATRICK'S PURGATORY?

This sanctuary is located on an island in Lough Derg (or Lake Derg) in Donegal, Ireland and was the favorite place for Saint Patrick to retire for solitude. Thousands of pilgrims have visited the island for over a thousand years, taking part in penitential exercises which last for three days. But a remarkable by-product of this pilgrimage is the large number of marriages that happen either during the stay or shortly thereafter. (One could almost call it "Saint Valentine's Purgatory"!)

WHY IS SAINT JOSEPH OF ARIMATHEA ASSOCIATED WITH THE HOLY GRAIL?

We know of Saint Joseph as the wealthy friend of Jesus who gave his tomb for Christ's burial. Legend has it that Joseph was exiled from the Holy Land for being a Christian and that he came to England, bringing with him the cup that was used at the Last Supper. The cup was subsequently lost, and King Arthur and the Knights of the Round Table devoted themselves to finding it—the search for the Holy Grail.

The English also believed that Joseph owned tin mines in England. It was thought that he was actually Jesus' uncle and that on a trip to inspect his mines, Joseph once brought his ten-year-old nephew with him! Later, in exile, it is said that Joseph visited Wearyall Hill in Glastonbury. According to tradition, it was here that he thrust his thornwood staff into the ground, where it took root and bloomed every Christmas Eve, which was then January 5. In 1752, the English calendar was set back eleven days to put Britain in line with other countries on the Gregorian calendar. Remarkably, the thornwood continued to blossom on the new date of Christmas Eve (December 24), proof, said some, that December 25 was the true birthday of Christ.

WHO ARE SOME MODERN-DAY SAINTS?

Two holy men come to mind immediately: Saint Maximilian Kolbe and Saint Joseph Moscati. The lives of these men were completely different, but their love of God and of others qualifies them both to be among the ranks of the saints.

SAINT MAXIMILIAN KOLBE

Saint Maximilian Kolbe was born of poor parents in 1894 in the town of Zdunska Wola, Poland. When he was a little boy, he had a vision of Mary holding out two crowns to him: one was white, signifying purity; and the other, red, signifying martyrdom. After Maximilian accepted the crowns, the Virgin smiled tenderly and disappeared.

As a young man, he obtained doctorates in philosophy and sacred theology from the Pontifical Gregorian University in Rome. But when he returned to Poland, he began a simple life, publishing *The Knight of the Immaculata*, a free magazine distributed to lay Catholics. The magazine became so successful that Maximilian and his fellow brothers built a friary, named Niepolalanow or "the property of Mary," and a printing press on land donated by a local prince. By 1938, it was the largest friary in the world, with more than eight hundred brothers who printed eleven publications and operated a radio station.

After the Nazis invaded Poland in 1939, Father Kolbe asked many of the brothers to leave because the friary was in the path of the invading German army. He remained, however, taking in as many as three thousand people a day, ensuring they were clothed, fed, and cared for. Then on February 17, 1941, Father Kolbe's press was halted, and he was arrested for treason by the Nazis. He was sent to Pawiak prison and was later transferred to Auschwitz.

In August 1941, his cell block was assembled before the deputy commander to be told that ten of them would die of starvation because a prisoner had escaped. One of the ten chosen, a Polish army sergeant, began to sob. He was forty years old and had a wife and children. Immediately, Father Kolbe made a bold request to the guard: "I wish to die in the place of this prisoner." Father Kolbe survived the two weeks in the starvation bunker and was finally given a lethal injection of carbolic acid on August 14, 1941. Pope John Paul II declared Maximilian Kolbe his own spiritual hero and granted him sainthood on November 9, 1982.

SAINT JOSEPH MOSCATI

Joseph Moscati was born in Benevento, Italy, in 1880. He was one of nine children who grew up in a home filled with love and piety. In 1892, Joseph's older brother was thrown from a horse and suffered a head injury, resulting in severe seizures. As Joseph spent many hours by his ailing brother's side, he began to think about dedicating his life to help the sick and poor.

Joseph graduated from the University of Naples with a medical degree in August 1903. He chose to do hospital work, but he also became well known for his research and lectures as a university professor and for the many articles he wrote. But his heart was always with those who were suffering. He would arise at five each morning, attend mass, and then walk to the nearby alleys to visit the poor and sick, all before beginning his daily work at the hospital.

At age thirty-nine, Joseph was appointed head physician in the hospital for incurables, and he continued his visits as before. Often when he called upon poor people, he would not only refuse payment for his services, but he would leave money for them either under a pillow or folded inside a prescription. He would not accept money for treating any priests and would encourage them to always be faithful to their calling. In fact, he considered entering the priesthood himself, but came to recognize that he was doing God's will in his own way. However, Joseph did make a vow of chastity, to which he was faithful his entire life, and committed himself to prayer and humility. He once told his students that it was better to look at a crippled lady who could not help the deformity than to gaze at a ravishing woman whose heart was corrupted. His diagnostic talent became known worldwide, and he would often be called upon to tend famous people.

All the work he did for the sick and poor began to take a toll on his health. But he refused to rest and continued on with his work as usual. It was a severe shock to all who knew him when they heard of his death. Joseph had been about his daily routine on April 12, 1927, and had felt unwell in the afternoon. Taking a short rest in his chair, he closed his eyes and died a sudden, peaceful death, which he had often said was a blessing to those who were prepared. People from all over came to pay their respects at his funeral, including the poor and the rich, and religious, political, and civil figures.

Claims have been made since his death that he continues to help those who pray to him. Some have seen him standing beside their beds; others have had spontaneous healing. On October 25, 1987, Pope John Paul II canonized Saint Joseph Moscati before thousands at a ceremony in Saint Peter's Square.

WHO ARE SOME "SAINTS-TO-BE"?

The Bishops' Synod of Rome in 1987 was given the task of examining the role of lay people in the present-day Roman Catholic Church. Some of their causes for canonization are being favorably considered, and many may shortly be declared saints. Among them is Blessed Kateri Tekakwitha, a Native American known as Lily of the Mohawks.

Blessed Kateri Tekakwitha was born in 1656 in what is now New York State. Her mother was an Algonquin who had been baptized by Jesuit missionaries, and her father was a Mohawk chief. When she was four years old, her parents and siblings died of smallpox, and Kateri suffered partial blindness and disfiguring facial marks from the disease. Her aunts and uncles brought her up, treating her no better than a slave girl due to her mother's professed faith.

When she was nearing her teens, Kateri met some Jesuit missionaries who preached in her village. Although she was drawn to Christianity, Kateri wasn't baptized until 1676, when she was twenty years old, taking the name Kateri after her patron saint, Saint Catherine of Alexandria. Life continued to be hard for her, and one of the missionaries suggested that she should move to the Saint Francis Xavier mission at Sault Saint-Louis. This village had been set up to help Christian natives who found it difficult to practice their religion in their communities. There she was adopted by Anastasia Tegonhatsiongo, who had originally come from Kateri's home village.

Kateri's piety soon became known throughout the settlement. She would attend two masses daily, staying in the church all day on Sundays and feast days. Her work was always performed cheerfully, and she would eagerly help others. Finally, in 1679, Kateri made a vow of perpetual virginity and consecrated herself to the Blessed Virgin. Others in the community began to seek her out for counseling and to imitate her life. Kateri began to suffer from blinding headaches and soon became confined to her sleeping shelf. On April 17, 1680, after receiving the Sacrament of the Sick, she died quietly.

After her death, several people were visited by her in visions. Father Chauchetière, who preached at Sault Saint-Louis, was shown by Kateri images of an overturned church and a native burnt at the stake. And several years later the church was blown over, and an Indian from the settlement did suffer that terrible death. Cures, both physical and spiritual, became so numerous that their occurrences became a way of life in the community. Her story appears in more than ten languages, and her relics are carefully preserved on the Mohawks of Kahnawake Reserve, located just south of the island of Montréal. On June 22, 1980, Kateri Tekakwitha, the Lily of the Mohawks, was declared blessed.

Of course, not all saints-in-the-making are laypersons. One of the most popular holy figures in this century was Padre Pio, a Capuchin friar from Italy. It was believed during his lifetime that he could be at two or more places at once, "read" the hearts of the people who came to see him, and heal the sick.

He lived in a mountaintop monastery in Italy, where thousands of people would wait hours to see him celebrate mass, to have him hear their confessions, or to touch his habit. Up until his death in 1968, he was receiving five thousand letters a month. In fact, his following was so great that Church authorities have tried to keep him hidden from the public to avoid spontaneous veneration of his sainthood. But his pictures still adorn the walls in many private homes and the dashboards of vehicles in Italy.

Padre Pio was born Francesco Forgiones on September 15, 1889, in Pietrelcina, southeast Italy. His family was poor, but deeply religious. Francesco grew up in the company of the Virgin Mary and the saints, who were simply considered to be part of his family. He was known as beautiful Francis, apparently for his appearance as much as for his behavior. On the family farm, he helped tend the sheep, and was aided by his guardian angel, whom he referred to as the companion of his youth.

When Francesco was ten years old, he announced that he wanted to be a friar. Once his father assured himself that the child was totally sincere, Papa Forgiones left for America, where he could make enough money to send the child to a private school that would prepare his son for the friary. When Francesco's studies were complete, he entered the Order of the Friars Minors, Capuchin, in 1903, taking the name of Pio.

There are many stories about the supernatural abilities of Padre Pio. On the evening of January 20, 1936, Padre Pio requested that the two laymen who were visiting him kneel down and pray for the soul of one who was soon to pass on. He afterward told them that they had just prayed for the king of England. Later that night around midnight, Pio entered the room of a young padre, saying, "Let us pray for a soul which at this moment is to appear before the tribunal of God—the king of England."[18] King George V died at 11:55 p.m., January 20, 1936, after a lethal injection of cocaine and morphine, given by his physician. Pio had no prior knowledge of the gravity of the king's sickness.

The signs of the stigmata appeared on Pio's body in August and September of 1918. Pio tried to hide the painful lesions for as long as possible, but eventually his brothers caught a glimpse of the bleeding wounds. Padre Pio later told of receiving the stigmata:

> All of a sudden, a great light shone round about my eyes. In the midst of this light there appeared the wounded Christ. He said nothing to me before he dis-appeared. [The crucifix in the choir transformed itself] into a great Exalted Being, all blood, from whom there came forth beams of lights with shafts of flames that wounded me in the hands and feet. My side had already been wounded on the fifth of August of the same year.[19]

Padre Pio died in the wee hours of September 23, 1968, almost fifty years to the day that the signs of the stigmata appeared on his body. It is estimated that over one hundred thousand people attended his funeral. Since then, thousands have visited the burial place of Pio and healings have been claimed. The process for his Cause of Canonization was opened on March 20, 1983.

WHICH SAINTS WERE MOST POPULAR WITH ARTISTS?

The saint who has been portrayed perhaps more than any-one else is Saint Nicholas. He was not only an extremely popular artistic subject in the Middle Ages, but in his role as Santa Claus (Father Christmas, Kris Kringle, Sinter Klaes), he appears in many different styles on Christmas cards, holiday favors, clothing—the list is endless. His image is one that almost everyone in the Western world can identify.

If you wander around the great museums, it's hard not to notice the seemingly endless portrayals of Saint Sebastian, pierced with arrows. Although this was not his martyrdom (legend states he survived the arrows and had to be clubbed to death), this scene has been one of the most painted in Western art. Among the artists who have portrayed Saint Sebastian are Titian and Bellini.

The other saint who was favored by medieval painters is Catherine of Alexandria. She has been depicted receiving a ring from the infant Jesus, preparing for her martyrdom on the wheel, and converting the philosophers. Raphael was one famous painter who depicted her.

WHAT MOVIES ARE THERE ABOUT SAINTS?

A number of movies have been made about the lives of the more popular saints. Here's a selected list:

Title	Subject
The Song of Bernadette (1943)	Saint Bernadette of Lourdes
Joan of Arc (1948)	Saint Joan of Arc
The Miracle of Our Lady of Fatima (1952)	The Virgin Mary

Saint Joan (1957)	Saint Joan of Arc
The Big Fisherman (1959)	Saint Peter
Francis of Assisi (1961)	Saint Francis of Assisi
Bernadette of Lourdes (1962)	Saint Bernadette of Lourdes
The Reluctant Saint (1962)	Saint Joseph of Cupertino
Trial of Joan of Arc (1962)	Saint Joan of Arc
Becket (1964)	Saint Thomas à Becket
And Now Miguel (1966)	Saint Isadore the Farmer
A Man for All Seasons (1966)	Saint Thomas More
Civilization: The Great Thaw (1970)	Saint Bernard of Clairvaux
Brother Sun, Sister Moon (1973)	Saint Francis of Assisi
A Time for Miracles (1980)	Saint Elizabeth Seton
Peter and Paul (1981)	Saints Peter and Paul
Thérèse (1986)	Saint Thérèse of Lisieux

ARE THERE ANY HISTORICAL FICTION WRITINGS ON SAINTS?

One can certainly find a great deal written about saints, and their lives and legends, but not as much historical fiction as one might expect. Author Taylor Caldwell wrote two novels: *Great Lion of God*, which was about the life of Saint Paul; and *Dear and Glorious Physician*, which told the story of Saint Luke. Both are interesting reading. There is also T. S. Eliot's "Murder in the Cathedral," a poetic dramatization of the death of Saint Thomas à Becket.

CHAPTER TEN

DO OTHER RELIGIONS HAVE SAINTS?

O my Lord, if I worship Thee for fear of hell, burn me in hell; and if I worship Thee for hope of Paradise, exclude me thence; but if I worship Thee for Thine own sake, withhold not from me Thine eternal beauty. AMEN.

—Rabi'a al-'Adawiyya (8th century Sufi woman)

Every religion has its own holy men and women to whom followers look as examples of virtue and piety. But only Roman Catholicism has a set of regulations as to what does and does not constitute a saint. In all other religions, saints are venerated by public acclamation, their burial sites become places of pilgrimage and often, of healing, and their stories are remembered down through the ages. We know them because of their love for God and for their fellow man.

JUDAISM

During the Crusades (around about 1090), Jewish communities in the Rhineland often committed mass suicide to escape death at the hands of the Christians. The memories of these martyrs are preserved in poetry and memorial books which were read in the synagogues. In addition, the Jewish community admired the leaders of the *Hasidei Ashkenaz* ("pious ones of Germany"), a mystical movement which developed out of the violence of the Crusades. The Hasid were an ascetic group of men who sought a simple way of life, eventually becoming saintlike figures.

But it is in North Africa that we find the most Jewish saints, or *zaddikim*. Most zaddikim are rabbis, teachers of Jewish communities. And traditionally, all rabbis have been men, for only males were once allowed to study the mysteries of the Torah, Jewish scripture and law.

One of the best-known zaddikim is Rabbi Amran ben Divan, who died in 1782. Pilgrims approach his tomb on the anniversary of his death and, after undergoing purification, remove their shoes, light candles, kiss the tomb, eat a meal, and petition the zaddik for help.

Pilgrimages are also made to other tombs, and in celebration of God, festivities often surround these events. The festival for Rabbi Simeon bar Yohai is still celebrated at his grave in Galilee on Lag b'Omer, the twenty-third day after Passover. The occasion is marked by joyful singing and dancing at the gravesite, lighting torches and bonfires, and performing special symbolic rites such as cutting children's hair.

Early each spring, thousands of people gather to participate in a pilgrimage to a cemetery in Beersheba, Israel, where Rabbi Chayim Chouri is buried. Since 1955, his tomb has become a shrine for his devoted followers. Rabbi Chouri was a pious, learned man in his lifetime and a very popular spiritual leader. But it wasn't until after his death that miracles were reported. Women now place food and drink on his grave so that they might absorb the healing powers. Candles are lit, picnics are spread on neighboring tombs, pilgrims buy portraits of the rabbi, and singing and dancing break out spontaneously. But, most of all, people pray for Rabbi Chayim Chouri's intervention in their lives.

ISLAM

Muslim holy men and women who have dedicated their lives to the quest of mystical reunion with God are called *Sufis*. The name comes from the Arabic word *suf*, which means wool. Toward the end of the eighth century, pious Muslims desiring a life of simplicity started to wear wool instead of the more elegant silk. Many of these people, whose lives were later held up as examples of pious living, became the "saints" of Islam, known as *wali*. Farid al-Din Attar, who lived in the early 1200s, wrote the *Memorial of the Saints* as a tribute and a history of the wali.

But not all Islamic walis were a part of the Sufi movement. One of the most interesting is Mohammed Ibn Idris al-Shafii, who was born in A.D. 768 in Gaza, and died in A.D. 820 in Cairo, Egypt. He had memorized the Koran by age seven, was qualified to make legal judgments at age fifteen, and spent his adult years as a celebrated jurist and teacher. After his death, he was buried in a southern cemetery in Cairo and then a large domed chamber was built over his tomb. For centuries, pilgrims from around the world have visited his burial place with petitions for the saint's intercession. People have also written letters to him throughout the ages. Most of these requests are for vengeance against injustices that the sender has suffered, but there are a good number asking for the cure of diseases, especially blindness.

In Islam, there is also a belief that a hierarchy of Islamic saints exists: one group whom Muslims believe help govern the world; and another special group who make up Allah's court. One Muslim writer states that God has appointed saints as . . .

> . . . the governors of the universe; they have become entirely devoted to His business, and have ceased to follow their sensual affections. Through the blessing of their advent the rain falls from heaven, and through the purity of their lives the plants spring up from the earth, and through their spiritual influence the Moslems gain victories over the unbelievers."[20]

BUDDHISM

As in Christianity, there are a number of Buddhist sects, or divisions of worship, and depending on the sect, Buddhist holy people may be called *arahants* or *bodhisattvas*. Much like the Christian saints, Buddhist holy people might lead lives of service, disowning all worldly possessions and performing miracles. And some Buddhist writings urge laypeople not only to venerate these holy individuals, but also to use them as models to imitate.

In northern modern Thailand, a number of "forest monks" have established forest hermitages, where they live ascetic, meditative lives. One of the most famous of these monks was Acharn Man, who was born in 1870 and died in 1943. He wandered in and out of the forests of Laos and northern Thailand, teaching laypeople and meditating. Listed among his accomplishments was his ability to pacify wild animals by communicating to them in a nonverbal language. After his death and cremation, Acharn Man's ashes were collected and distributed as relics. Reportedly, grains of his ashes turned into crystals and precious jewels. Today amulets stamped with his image are blessed by his disciples and widely distributed to laypeople.

Many saints and mystics have emerged from the religious richness of India. One of these holy people, the Guru Padma Sambhava, is considered second only to Buddha in the Himalayan region. Legends about him reveal that he was a great missionary and teacher, and he performed miraculous feats. He believed that a religion should not be forced on a people, but that a preacher should win over their hearts, ensuring all the while that their original culture not be disturbed. He promoted the building of many Buddhist temples, and many other monasteries were built at holy sites visited by Guru Padma Sambhava or blessed by him.

Just as Christians invoke saints to help them in their daily lives, devotees in Sri Lanka invoke Buddhist saints for help in solving puzzles and dealing with the conflicts of everyday life. The custom of asking saints to assist with concerns—such as finding a husband, a job, or a precious lost object—crosses religious boundaries.

HINDUISM

Lists of Hindu saints began appearing as early as the eighth century, and by the eleventh and twelfth centuries, stories of their lives were being written. One of the oldest and best-known works is the *Bhaktamal*, which seems to have been written in the early 1700s. Among the many saints discussed is Mira Bai, who is the best known of the medieval singer-saints in India today. The songs she wrote are sung throughout the country. She is represented as a heroine in many of India's feature films.

Mira was a Rajput princess who was so absorbed in the love of Krishna, a Hindu deity, that she understood that she was his wife. Her subsequent earthly marriage was, at best, of secondary importance. Ashamed and humiliated, her family tried to poison her, but the vile liquid only made her glow with greater health and happiness. Her singing became more animated and beautiful than before. She proved herself to be fearless in the face of adversity and death, a shining example for all to follow. Her life on earth ended when Krishna drew her up into heaven with him, and she was never seen again.

CONFUCIANISM

Can we call a Confucian sage a saint? Sages are expected to live exemplary lives, forsaking worldly goods and becoming humble, gentle, and self-effacing. One of the least-known features of the Confucian philosophy is the temple. In these sacred spaces, rituals venerate Confucius (the Chinese philosopher who founded Confucianism in the fifth century B.C.), his selected disciples, and some noteworthy Confucians throughout the centuries.

In A.D. 59, the Chinese emperor Ming-ti recognized Confucius as the patron of literature, or *wen*. It follows then, that Confucius may be considered the patron saint of scholars.

HAITIAN VOODOO

Haitian Voodoo is a mixture of Catholicism and various African religious traditions and was first practiced on the plantations of Haiti. The voodoo spirits have both Catholic saint names and Afro-Haitian names. Their feast days are approximately the same as well. Thus, Dambala, the snake spirit, is also known as Saint Patrick, who is said to have driven snakes from Ireland. Dambala's feast day is celebrated around March 17. Likewise, Azaka's (Saint Isidore's) feast day is celebrated in May; Ogou's (Saint James the Elder's) is in July; and Ghede's (Saint Gerard's), in November. On these feast days, praying, singing, and dancing go on from morning to night in front of a table laden with the food and drink each saint favors. The celebrants usually ask the spirits for help with problems in their lives.

WERE ANY SAINTS FROM OTHER RELIGIONS VENERATED IN CHRISTIANITY?

Perhaps the most interesting case of veneration of a non-Christian saint involves Saint Josaphat, who was widely venerated in the Middle Ages. According to Lawrence Cunningham, the author of *The Meaning of Saints*, Saint Josaphat was actually the Buddha. Cunningham claims that stories of the Buddha came to Europe from the trade routes of the East, or perhaps from crusaders returning home from the Holy Land, and were intermingled to create a story about the life of an Eastern saint named Josaphat. The name is likely to be a corruption of Bodhisattva, one of the titles of the Buddha.

Scholars also tell us that the prophet Isaiah and the Jewish martyrs known as the Maccabees were venerated as Christian saints until recently. The Apocrypha (1 Macc. 7:17) tells the story of Judas Maccabaeus and his brothers, who seemingly singlehandedly routed pagan oppressors from Israel and ultimately died for their cause: "The bodies of thy saints were scattered, their blood was shed round Jerusalem, and there was none to bury them."

The early Christians accepted these Jewish saints into their own calendar, giving them a feast day of August 1. It was not until 1960, during the revision of the Roman calendar, that these saints and the Prophet Isaiah lost their veneration in Roman Catholicism.

CHAPTER ELEVEN

ARE THERE MANY WOMEN SAINTS?

You, O eternal Trinity, are a deep sea, into which the more I enter the more I find, and the more I find the more I seek. The soul cannot be satiated in your abyss, for she continually hungers after you, the eternal Trinity, desiring to see you with the light of your light. As the hart desires the springs of living water, so my soul desires to leave the prison of this dark body and see you in truth.

O abyss, O eternal Godhead, O sea profound, what more could you give me than yourself? You are the fire that ever burns without being consumed; you consume in your heat all the soul's self-love; you are the fire which takes away cold; with your light you illuminate me so that I may know all your truth. Clothe me, clothe me with yourself, eternal truth, so that I may run this mortal life with true obedience, and with the light of your most holy faith. AMEN.

—Saint Catherine of Siena
(14th century)

There are a number of women saints in Christianity: Saint Anne, Saint Joan of Arc, and Saint Catherine of Siena—just to name a few. Echoing Pythagoras's belief that "women as a sex are more naturally akin to piety,"[21] most other major religions have also honored their holy women.

CHRISTIANITY

The early Church considered men and women equal before God. In some areas women were made deacons, preaching and teaching as their male counterparts did. Roughly at the same time the first monasteries were founded, convents for women were also established. At first, during the age of persecution, the Church instituted a special vow for the consecration of virginity to be observed by girls who were old enough to be married, while living with their families. Later, convents were set up to provide the devoted with quiet and seclusion. The sister of Saint Antony the Hermit established the first of these around A.D. 271 in Middle Egypt. A number of women who lived their lives in such convents became canonized by the Church. One such woman was Saint Brigid or Saint Bride, who became a patron saint of Ireland.

Brigit was born into a life of servitude, tending sheep, grinding corn, and washing the feet of guests at her father's command. Brigit's father thought she was excessively generous because she was always giving away his possessions to those in need. Once while her father was petitioning the king of Leinster to use his daughter's services, Brigit gave away his most valued possession, a jeweled sword, to a passing leper. On hearing of her actions, the king of Leinster prevailed upon Brigit's father to free her from servitude. Her father agreed and ensured that Brigit became educated, making her childhood commitment to become a nun a reality.

Traveling throughout Ireland, Brigit founded convent settlements, which were centers of religious and lay learning, teaching craftsmanship and practical skills in farming, harvesting, milling, dyeing, weaving, and caring for the sick. She loved gaiety, humor, festive gatherings, and music, and she encouraged them in her communities. It is interesting that she is not accredited with performing great miracles, but instead took a practical course. In an age when bathing was considered a luxury, she advocated cleanliness as a means of preventing illness. Often her cures were preceded by an order to cleanse the sick person.

The most famous of her settlements was in Leinster, where she built for herself a cell of intertwined reeds and clay in the shade of an oak tree. It was called *kill-dara*, the church of the oak. The community is now known as Killdare, a major center for learning in Ireland. Brigit died on February 1, A.D. 525, and was buried in the same tomb as Saint Patrick.

HINDUISM

No other scripture has given women such equality with men as the *Vedas* of the Hindus:

> The wife and husband being the equal halves of one substance are equal in every respect; therefore both should join and take equal parts in all work, religious and secular.[22]

In ancient India, women commonly acquired knowledge and spirituality. And many achieved such a high degree of spirituality that records of their lives have survived through the ages. One such figure is Avvaiyar, one of the greatest women of historical India.

It is said that Avvaiyar was orphaned as a little child and was found and brought up by a poet. At the age of sixteen, she became famous for her beauty, and many kings asked for her hand in marriage. But Avvaiyar was deeply devoted to religious and literary pursuits and wanted to serve people. She prayed for peace from all the pressures that her beauty created. God heard her request and transformed her into an old woman with a common appearance.

Traveling around India, the Universal Grandmother, as she was called, imparted her vision to one and all. Kings sought her out for her wisdom, but Avvaiyar would avoid them, preferring a simple life among the poor. She died at an old age, leaving behind many ethical writings, some of which are studied today by students in India. Here's an example of her work:

> Harsh words do not conquer soft ones; the arrow that strikes down elephants harms not a piece of cotton; the rock that is not split with the long iron crowbar, splits when the roots of a tender shrub enter it.[23]

BUDDHISM

The Buddha declared during the course of his life that the Dharma, or The Way (a set of customs and laws for living), was for everyone, regardless of their caste, class, or sex. He established one order for monks and one for nuns, with all novices receiving the same education. However, nuns did rank below the monks, and strict rules were established to dictate their conduct.

Ambapali, one of the greatest Buddhist women saints, lived as a wealthy prostitute at the time of the Buddha. During the wanderings of Lord Buddha and his disciples, she came up to him, bowed, and sat near to him, learning the Dharma. The next day, she invited him to her luxurious house and, after dinner, gave him all that she owned. The remainder of her life was spent serving the poor and trying to achieve purity of mind. Ambapali serves as a reminder to us all that no matter how we may have behaved in the past, we always have the ability to change our lives for the better.

ISLAM

Sufis were among the earliest Muslim saints, and there are a number of women in their ranks. Rabi'a al-'Adawiyya is one of the most celebrated of the early Sufis and her teachings are referred to even today.

Rabi'a was born in Basra (Iraq) in A.D. 717. Her parents were very poor but religious. At a young age, she was orphaned and left to roam the streets of Basra, where she was captured and sold into slavery. Her master worked her very cruelly, but Rabi'a never lost her faith. She fasted during the day while she carried out her duties and prayed to God during the night. One night, her master awoke from sleep to see her in deep contemplation. A lamp was suspended in midair over her head, lighting up the entire house. He was so surprised, he freed her the next morning.

Rabi'a was now able to lead a life of complete devotion to God. Soon word of her asceticism and mysticism spread. Many came to listen to her teachings and seek her advice. Once when a man asked her to pray for him, she replied,

"Who am I? Obey your Lord and pray to Him, for He will answer the supplicant when he prays." Some of Rabi'a's students were rich and powerful, and offered her financial assistance, but she refused it. She died in A.D. 801 and was buried in Basra. Although she was unschooled in spiritual matters, she had opened her heart to her God to receive His Light. Her path to her God was a practical one, which could be followed step-by-step by the devoted. And her inspirational works have been revered by almost all great Sufi writers.

JUDAISM

Because traditionally women could not become rabbis, as of yet there are no "official" women zaddikim, or Jewish saints. But here is the story of one Jewish woman who certainly seems deserving of the title.

Henrietta Szold was born in Baltimore, Maryland, in 1860, the eldest daughter of Rabbi Benjamin Szold and his wife, Sophia. Because Rabbi Szold had no sons, he gave his eldest child the education and training usually reserved for boys at that time. After excelling in her high school studies, Henrietta taught and wrote to help bring in extra money to feed the family.

In 1882, thousands of Jews fled Russia, a number of whom found their way to Baltimore. Henrietta set up a school for them, instructing them on how to become integrated into their new society. At the age of thirty-three, she left teaching, moved to Philadelphia, and took the post of literary secretary at the Jewish Publication Society of America, which she held for twenty-three years. In order to prepare for her work, she studied the Talmud at the Jewish Theological Seminary of America, which had never before allowed a woman to enter its premises.

During a visit to Palestine in 1909, Henrietta was devastated by the plight of Jewish colonists attempting to eke out a meager living on the harsh land. Children suffered from malnutrition and blindness. Henrietta, determined to establish health and social welfare services for all of Palestine—Jews and Arabs alike—organized fund-raisers back in the United States. Soon she was able to send trained nurses to help the people of Palestine. During World War I, she traveled to the Holy Land and realized her dream by creating and supervising the development of Palestine's social health service. She introduced the school meal system, opened a health center in Jerusalem and a hospital in Tel-Aviv, and became a member of the National Assembly. She also brought thousands of poor, abandoned, and orphaned children from many countries and organized their care, rehabilitation, and education.

At the age of seventy-five, Henrietta felt called to undertake another immense project. Beginning in 1934, when thousands of Jewish children were displaced by Nazi orders, Henrietta and her helpers cared for and educated orphans from all over the world. In her last year of life, at age eighty-four, she continued to meet "her children," sit by their cots at night, and teach them new songs. She died on February 13, 1945, the foster mother of over sixty thousand children! She had lived to see many of her goals realized: the opening of the Hadassah University Medical Center on Mount Scopus in 1939, the Henrietta Szold Nurses' School, and the establishment of over fifty welfare stations for prenatal and infant care. "I am a happy person," were her last words.

WHO WAS THE FIRST WOMAN SAINT?

No scholarly sources identify any one woman as "the first woman saint." Is it the Virgin Mary, whose cult sprang up around the fifth century throughout Europe? Or perhaps it's Saint Anne, Mary's mother, or Saint Mary Magdalene, or her sister, Saint Martha. What about Saint Agatha and Saint Cecilia, whose martyrdoms are said to have taken place in the third century? Saint Appollonia was martyred in A.D. 249, but the Church reduced her cult to local status as of 1969. We don't even know for certain who was the first woman to be venerated. But we do know that many women have played a significant part in the development and nurturing of religions around the world. For that alone, all should be honored.

ARE THERE ANY MARRIED WOMEN SAINTS?

There are a number of women saints who were married. Many of them, like Saints Monica and Elizabeth Ann Seton, were widowed while still young, but others lived out their lives happily married. One of these was Saint Margaret, Queen of Scotland in the eleventh century.

Margaret was born of royal blood in Hungary and at an early age yearned for the religious life. She was diverted from the convent by King Malcolm of Scotland, who fell in love with her at a chance meeting and asked Margaret's father for her hand. Queen Margaret brought joy to the king and his kingdom, gaily decorating his gloomy castles and teaching the king to pray and to show mercy to the poor. Her influence was so persuasive that the raiding warrior repented his sins and became so devout that his name is included among the saints in some Scottish calendars.

Queen Margaret bore the king six sons and two daughters, all of whom were known for their piety and good deeds. Often the king and queen spent the nights together in prayer, and Margaret would attend five or six masses. Then she would wait upon twenty-four poor people who were dependent upon her support before she ate her own frugal meal. The king and queen died within days of each other; he in battle and she in prayer.

Other married women saints of note include: Saint Mechtildis, empress of Germany; Saint Blanche of Castile, queen of France (mother of Saint Louis); Saint Elizabeth (or Isabel), queen of Portugal; Saint Elizabeth, queen of Hungary; Saint Hedwig (or Jadwiga) of Poland; Saint Jeanne de Chantal; and Saint Catherine of Genoa.

IS THE VIRGIN MARY A SAINT?
The Virgin Mary has long been regarded by the Christian Church as having special status, a little higher than a saint and therefore, closer to God. The reverence and homage paid to her is called *hyperdulia*, which is distinguished from

the adoration of God, *latria*, and the honor paid to the saints and angels, *dulia*. From ancient times, Mary has been venerated under the title of "God-bearer" (*Theotokos*). Her cult increased substantially after the Council of Ephesus in A.D. 431, which stated that Mary is the Mother of Jesus and is, therefore, the Mother of God.

We know very little of Mary's life, however. She is mentioned several times in the New Testament, including her presence at the Crucifixion. But we know nothing of her later years or of her death. From the fifth century on, some Christians have believed that Mary remained a virgin all her life, and that her body was taken directly into heaven (the Assumption). In 1854, the Roman Catholic Church proclaimed that she was conceived and born without original sin, which is known to many as the Immaculate Conception. Among her many titles are: Mother of God, Ever Virgin, Highly Favored Daughter, Our Lady of the Immaculate Conception, Our Lady of the Rosary, Blessed Mother, Mother of the Church, and Our Lady of Lourdes. The Virgin Mary's main feast days are as follows:

Motherhood	January 1
Our Lady of Lourdes	February 11
The Annunciation	March 25
Visit to Elizabeth	May 31
Our Lady of Mount Carmel	July 16
The Assumption (the principal feast)	August 15
Queenship	August 22
Birthday	September 8
Sorrows	September 15
Our Lady of Ransom	September 24
The Holy Rosary	October 7

Presentation   November 21
The Immaculate Conception   December 8

The most popular Marian devotion is the rosary, a mental or vocal prayer involving meditation on the lives of Mary and Jesus. A rosary is also a necklace of beads used to keep track of the number of prayers recited.

ARE THERE PATRON SAINTS JUST FOR WOMEN?

Many saints serve as patrons for special issues and circumstances that concern women. Here are a few examples.

BREASTFEEDING: SAINT GILES

According to tradition, while Saint Giles was a hermit in southern France, he would drink milk from a female red deer, thus leading to his patronage of breastfeeding. He was one of the most popular saints during the Middle Ages.

CHILDBIRTH: SAINT RAYMOND NONNATUS

Saint Raymond Nonnatus (meaning "not-born") was born by Cesarean section after his mother died in childbirth, hence his patronage. He is also invoked by midwives, children, and pregnant women.

HOUSEWIVES: SAINT MARTHA

Saint Martha, the sister of Lazarus, is best known for her graciousness and hospitality while Jesus visited her home and for serving dinner to Jesus just a few days before the Crucifixion.

MOTHERHOOD: THE VIRGIN MARY

Probably the most obvious patronage, the Blessed Virgin Mary is the patron saint for motherhood. As the Mother of Jesus, she is considered to be the most powerful of all the saints and is invoked by mothers for their every need.

PREGNANCY: SAINT ANNE

Before the birth of her daughter, Mary, Saint Anne and her husband, Joachim, were childless for years. They prayed and fasted for forty days, during which time they both had an angelic vision assuring them that they would have a child. Anne later gave birth to Mary. Saint Anne thus has the responsibility for looking after pregnant women.

SINGLE WOMEN SEARCHING FOR HUSBANDS: SAINT AGNES

According to legend, Saint Agnes, the patron saint of young girls, was only thirteen years old when she was stabbed in the throat for professing her faith. She had refused to marry, declaring that she was already married to Christ and would die rather than lose her virginity. Over the years, the tradition arose that if a young girl observed a special ritual on Saint Agnes's Eve (January 20, her feast day being January 21), she would have a vision of her future husband. John Keats describes this ritual to some extent in his poem *The Eve of Saint Agnes*:

> They told her how, upon Saint Agnes' Eve,
> Young virgins might have visions of delight,
> And soft adorings from their loves receive

Upon the honeyed middle of the night,
If ceremonies due they did aright;
As, supperless to bed they must retire,
And couch supine their beauties, lily white;
Nor look behind, nor sideways, but require
Of Heaven with upward eyes for all that they desire.

(verses 46-54)

WIVES: SAINT MONICA

Saint Monica, mother of the great theologian, Saint Augustine, is the patron saint of wives. Due to her patience and love, she converted her husband, Patricius, to Christianity.

CHAPTER TWELVE

WHAT DO CHILDREN THINK OF SAINTS?

O God, make us children of quietness, and heirs of peace.

—*Saint Clement*

Children have perhaps the best view of the world. They have honest questions, seeking answers to things that adults, with their busy lives, have long since ceased to wonder about. And their simple approach is so refreshing. As we learn from the Gospel according to Matt. 18:1-4, children can provide adults with insight:

> At that time the disciples came to Jesus, saying, "Who is the greatest in the kingdom of heaven?" And calling to him a child, he put him in the midst of them, and said, "Truly, I say to you, unless you turn and become like children, you will never enter the kingdom of

heaven. Whoever humbles himself like this child, he is the greatest in the kingdom of heaven."

What do children think of saints? I asked many children this question, and after answering, they asked many questions in return. Let's hear from them.

CAMERON
(AGE 8)

Saints have to be good people all of their lives when they are alive. I don't think they do anything special after they're dead. But saints do go up to heaven, and there they do good things for God. Saints might help people here on earth. They might make people feel better.

Why can saints only be saints after they're dead?

That's a really good question, Cameron. We wait to call someone a saint until after they have died, so we can make sure that the person really did perform good deeds for his whole life. Sometimes a person is so good that people recognize them as being "just like a saint" when they're alive, such as Mother Teresa, who helps the poor and sick.

According to the Roman Catholic Church, a person cannot be called a saint unless he is dead. The pope is the only one who can say that someone is a saint. He does this by looking over the life of the person, seeing that he or she did good things and helped people if they were sick. It takes a long time to decide this, usually more than fifty years. This way the Church can make sure that the saint was always a good and helping person.

Why can't saints be angels, but angels can be saints?

We know that saints are people who have died and gone to heaven. They lived on the earth, just like you and me. They needed to eat and drink and sleep, and they most likely had a lot of questions just like yours! But angels never live on the earth like you and me. Since the time God created them, they have lived in heaven with Him. So you can see that saints can't be angels because they are human beings. There has been one exception to this. According to legend, Saint Francis of Assisi became Rhamiel, the Angel of Mercy, after he arrived in heaven.

But how then can angels become saints, you ask? Only three of the archangels are also called saints. They are Michael, Gabriel, and Raphael. These angels are the closest to us. It was Gabriel who told Mary that she would have a son called Jesus. Michael is the soldier angel, who fought with Satan and threw him out of heaven, and Raphael is the angel who heals people. Because they have been so helpful to humankind, it was decided that they were like the saints, so they were given the title. You might also like to know that there is a special day to celebrate all the guardian angels: it's October 2.

GRAHAM
(AGE 9)

I think that saints are good people who have died. They have done good things for people when they were alive and after they were dead. I heard the story of Saint Nicholas, who gave gold to the daughters of a poor man so that they could get married. He dropped it down the chimney.

Why do people call them saints?

Well, Graham, *saint* comes from a Latin word, *sanctus,* meaning holy. Latin is the language used by the ancient Romans who ruled much of the world that Jesus and His Apostles knew. Many of the words that we use today come from Latin.

When the Romans talked about people they thought of as being very good, or holy, they used the word *sanctus* to describe them. And then afterwards, the Christians used the same word to describe people they knew who had lived a good life—individuals they felt they could look up to. Eventually the word came into the English language as *saint.*

JEFF AND MARK
(AGES 8 AND 5)

We heard the word *saint* when we were in Ireland. We think they are leprechauns, like Saint Patrick. Maybe saints are four-leaf clovers. Saints can do things that other people can't do.

What did Saint Patrick do?

The most amazing thing that Saint Patrick did was to con-vert the people of Ireland to Christianity in about thirty years. And for that reason, Saint Patrick is the patron saint of Ireland, which means he looks after the people of Ireland. The Irish around the world celebrate his feast day on March 17.

There is a legend which says that Saint Patrick made all the snakes in Ireland leave and go into the ocean. Some peo-ple who are afraid of snakes will pray to Saint Patrick if they see one to help them get over their fears.

MATT
(AGE 7)

I think that a saint is someone who is very special. And I think that he or she must be a very good person. There are a lot of saints, like Saint Nicholas and Saint John, but before you become a saint, you have to check and see if there is a day for you, like Saint Valentine's Day.

Is there a saint for me?

Well, Matt, there is a saint named Matthew. He was a tax collector for the Romans before Jesus invited him to be one of his disciples. And he wrote one of the books of the New Testament—the Gospel according to Matthew. There's no mention of him in the Bible after the death of Jesus, but some people think that he went to the East to tell people about Jesus. Because of his background, he is the patron saint of accountants, bankers, bookkeepers, and tax collectors. September 21 is Saint Matthew's Day, so you can celebrate it, if you like.

STEVEN
(AGE 8)

Saints are nice. They are people who love God and work for Him. They spread the Word of God and help people. I know that Bishop Romaro is a saint. He was killed a few years ago down in El Salvador. All the saints got killed, except for a couple who died from sickness, like Saint Dominic.

I prayed to Saint Anthony, and he found a pair of shorts for me and a comic book, too, I think.

Were any of the saints soldiers?

Yes, Steven, a number of the saints were soldiers at some point in their lives, although most resigned their positions in order to better do God's will. Among these were Saint Camillus of Lellis, who later helped the sick; Saint Ignatius of Loyola, who went on to found the Jesuit Order; and Saint Longinus, who stood beside the cross and pierced Jesus' side with his lance. According to tradition, Longinus had a malady of the eyes which was instantly cured when he rubbed them with the blood of Christ.

Saint Joan of Arc, on the other hand, was commanded by the voice of God to drive the enemies of France from the land. She, along with Saint Martin of Tours, Saint Sebastian, and Saint George, is a patron of soldiers. Perhaps the most powerful of all the soldiers is Saint Michael, the archangel who threw the devil out of heaven in a great battle.

CORRY
(AGE 8)

I don't know a lot about saints, so I would just like to ask a question:

What do saints do now?

Because saints are in heaven, it's hard for people to imagine that they do things here on earth. But many people believe that they do. There are stories of people not only being helped by a saint, but also of saints curing people when they are sick. Here's a short story of a man who visited the village of Saint Anne de Beaupré to talk to Saint Anne:

One day a man named William McNabb decided to visit [the village of] Saint Anne de Beaupré, because he had heard that miracles had happened there. He was suffering from very bad headaches and the doctors had wanted to do an operation on him. While he was praying during a church service, he started to cry and used his handkerchief to cover his eyes. When he looked down, he discovered the handkerchief was filled with blood! A man who was sitting beside him gave him his handkerchief. Mr. McNabb put this one over his eyes as well, but there wasn't any blood on this one. Mr. McNabb said that his pain went away and never returned.[24]

Mr. McNabb believed that Saint Anne had cured him of his headaches.

CHRIS
(AGE 13)

God sends saints down to people who are in need of help, like Saint Jude. If you're in trouble, and you need something, you pray to him, and if you do your part, he'll probably try to help you find things. There are all different kinds of saints; there are patron saints of cities, countries, and things like money.

My patron saint is Paul. I chose him to be my patron saint because he was the Apostle to the Gentiles, so I wanted to try and be like him and be an apostle, in a way. He traveled in and around Tarsus.

Does God send saints down to people who ask, or does God send saints down to people whom He thinks need help?

Well, Chris, I think that God actually does both. God will send us help whether we've asked for it or not. But sometimes we pray very, very hard for His help, and it doesn't seem that He's listening. Have you ever experienced anything like that? God always hears our prayers; He is always listening to us. But sometimes He knows that something that we want isn't the best thing for us after all, and so sometimes He silently says "No." And it seems like He hasn't listened, or that He hasn't sent a saint down to help us. But, just maybe, He sends a saint to help us get through a bad time, even if we aren't aware of it.

Is everyone named after a saint?

Not everyone is named after a saint, because people of other religions don't have the same traditions as the Roman Catholic Church. It is required that Catholics take a saint's name at their confirmation, as you did when you took the name of Paul. And many children are named after a saint when they are baptized. You were probably named after Saint Christopher, whose name means Christ-bearer.

KIM
(AGE 13)

I think saints are real people who are like us. They have been touched by God and do Christian things to help people. They're special people like Mother Teresa, who will probably be a saint one day because she helps the sick and the poor people. I chose Saint Mary Magdalene to be my confirmation saint because she gives me some hope. She was a sinner, but then she asked God to forgive her, and she changed her life completely around.

Why do some saints' bodies not decompose?
Who were these saints?

Science can't entirely answer why some saints' bodies do not decompose. Some people have speculated that the tomb in which the body has been laid is very dry, retarding the decaying process. But that cannot explain all cases. Perhaps the person is so good that their holiness shines through their bodies, changing it and making it incorruptible. We don't really know for sure, because it doesn't happen in all cases. For instance, the bodies of Saint Francis of Assisi, Saint Anthony of Padua, Saint John Bosco, and Saint Teresa of Laces all suffered decomposition. But we do know that the body of Saint Francis Xavier has been examined by physicians and declared to be incorruptible, as have been the bodies of Saint Rita of Cascia, Saint Bernadette Soubirous, and Saint Catherine Labouré. And it has also been known to happen to a few who will likely never be declared saints, such as Abraham Lincoln.

There was the case of a young girl in Ireland by the name of Mary Therese Collins. She was described by her friends as "radiant with goodness". On September 29, 1929, she calmly bid goodbye to her family and friends, saying that she would be dead by the morning. And sure enough, the next day she was found dead in her home. In 1981, another of Mary's family was to be buried in her grave. To the amazement of the grave diggers, Mary's coffin and body were intact. They said her hands were joined in prayer beneath her chin, and her eyes were open and "shining like diamonds". The site has now become a place of pilgrimage in Ireland, miraculous cures have been claimed, and there is now a movement afoot petitioning for her canonization.[25]

MELISSA
(AGE 13)

I think a saint is someone who is a guide for you, and whenever you need them they will always be there.

Whenever I've needed help, I guess I've never gone to a saint before, I've always prayed to God, but most of the time, whatever you wish for in a certain way does come true, and if it doesn't you just have to accept it.

Saints are people who care about people who are alive, and they put people in front of themselves. They are not selfish, and they're really in love with God. They are really nice people. I chose Saint Monica to be my patron saint, because she is the patron saint of married women and helped her son to return back to God. A lot of people don't care what their children believe in, and I would like to help other people with their faith.

How do you know that a saint is right for you?
Do you have to "stay" with the same saint?

I think that you've done everything you could to make sure your patron saint is right for you. You've read a lot about Saint Monica's life, and you've decided you'd like to pattern your life after hers. And it probably feels like she's the correct saint for you right now, wouldn't you say? You like what she did and what she stands for.

But nothing in our lives is written in stone. When you're older, you may see things a little bit differently. And, by all means, you're perfectly free to change your saint. You may not want to change your name, for Saint Monica may still mean a lot to you. But if you read about another saint's life and it touches your heart, don't be afraid to follow that saint's direction either. All the saints have a lot to teach us.

EMMY-JO
(AGE 13)

I feel that saints are more like role models for us young children, and they guide us to the right path in our religion and our faith. Some saints suffered in their lifetimes. Saints give us a lot of encouragement and help us through life. My saint is Maria Goretti. I picked her because she was pretty strong, because she had enough forgiveness in her heart to forgive the man who murdered her. Last year, my aunt passed away, and Maria Goretti gave me enough courage to look beyond the death to get over that. I know that the death was the best for her because then she would be living with God. My grandma's in the hospital right now, and she's also going through the same thing, so I think that Maria Goretti is watching over me.

What types of characteristics does a saint have to have?

Not only did Maria Goretti, while on her deathbed, forgive the man who murdered her, but she also appeared to him in a dream while he was in prison, offering flowers to him. From then on, he was a changed man, being assured of her forgiveness and her love for him. One of the most outstanding aspects of the saints is their unconditional love for their fellow man and their ability to forgive perceived wrongs. It is this love that brought Saint Francis of Assisi to kiss the face of a horribly disfigured man, thereby curing him of cancer, and today allows Mother Teresa to work in the terrible conditions of the Indian slums. And, of course, the saints love God absolutely. They give their lives completely to His purpose.

CATHERINE
(AGE 14)

Saints are people who do courageous acts so that they live in God's family. Most of them have died for what they have done. There was one boy whose father didn't want him to become a Catholic, so he chopped his head off. And there was a Mohawk Indian who became a Catholic, and she died.

SHEELAH
(AGE 14)

I've never seen a saint, but a few of my friends might be saints when they grow up. Saints seem to be just like us. They are kind and courageous and just really nice. They help people get through life, and they're also very happy and optimistic and look on the bright side of their world. They don't take anything for granted.

I chose Saint Patrick for my patron saint because I'm from Ireland, as well, and I thought what he did was really neat. He changed almost everyone in Ireland to Catholicism. He showed great leadership, and I liked that because I would like to be a leader when I grow up. I would like to change the world and make it a better place for people to live, so there will be no racism or stereotyping.

Saints are role models for me, so I can look up to someone. They also help to guide people through life. I look up to God, but it's really hard because I don't know what He or She is like, so it's easier to think of a human.

Will it take Mother Teresa less time than normal to become a saint?

It's very likely, Sheelah, that Mother Teresa will become a saint very shortly after she dies. She is probably the best-known religious figure in the world today, and there will be thousands of people who will petition for her to be sanctified. The rules are somewhat stringent—fifty years usually must elapse before a person can be beatified, and then two miracles must happen after the date of the beatification. But ultimately, the decision will rest with the pope. The rules have been waived for other people, and my feeling is that it might be the same for Mother Teresa.

AMANDA
(AGE 14)

A saint is someone who has done something which makes people look up to them. I think some people idolize them, so that they follow in their footsteps. I like Saint Bernadette because she was really nice to kids and people. She took care of people's kids. And she made a spring come out of the ground in the middle of a drought, and the spring is there today. I'd like to help people more, like Saint Bernadette.

ALYSSA
(AGE 13)

Saints teach us about what is right and wrong about life by setting an example for everyone. Different saints have different beliefs. My saint, Saint Stephen, helped people who were both Jewish and Catholic. He was Jewish himself, so he was discriminated against, just because of his religion. Just because you believe in a different religious tradition doesn't mean that you're different than everybody else. You should always help other people, no matter who they are or where they come from. Saint Stephen risked his life to help other people, just like Jesus did. Jesus didn't care what religious background people had or what town they came from, he helped everyone.

JEFF
(AGE 14)

Saints are people who have done miraculous things to help other people instead of themselves. A miracle happens through the help of God—I don't think it can just happen to anyone. It usually happens to someone who wants to do something good for other people. It's not like changing a frog into a bird or anything like that. I've seen shows where there are kids who are dying, and they've prayed and become well the next day. I guess that anyone can be a saint if he tries to help people and put others before himself. It would be neat to see Saint Jeff on the wall of a cathedral, but you'd have to have the opportunity to do good things, like stop the war in Bosnia. Maybe if you were outgoing and did things that other people wouldn't do, you might be recognized for that.

Why are schools named after saints?

Well, you've probably seen not only schools named after saints, like Saint Marguerite or Holy Family, but also hospitals and churches. When people get together and start planning the building of a hospital or school, it's an exciting time. The people may decide to put their new endeavor under the protection, or patronage, of a saint or saints who appeal to the majority. So when you see Saint Paul's Church, or Saint Joseph's Hospital, or Our Lady of Lourdes' School, you know that these saints have been assigned the task of looking over them. They are the patron saints of these places.

Why are some saints more popular than others?

Throughout history, some saints have been more popular than others. And a lot of it has to do with the times the people were living in. During times of war, such as the Hundred Years' War, Saint George became very popular in England, and has remained that country's patron saint. Some saints, known as the Fourteen Holy Helpers, were most popular during the outbreak of the Plague, because it was believed that they could be invoked for healing.

But I think that the most popular saints are those who are the most down-to-earth, whose loving and kind disposition endears them to generation after generation of people. Saint Francis of Assisi, who is portrayed as a very merry soul, is probably the most popular saint of all time. Some saints are well known locally, such as the patron saint of a nation or region. Some of our more famous saints, such as Saint Catherine and Saint Christopher, have been taken out of the calendar of saints, because there are no known facts about their lives. So, Saint Christopher, who is one of our more popular saints, may not be as well-known by people living in the next century.

WHO ARE THE PATRON SAINTS OF CHILDREN?

Children of all ages need guidance and protection as they face the world in their innocence. Here are a number of saints who can be called upon to help children.

BABIES: SAINT ZENO

Saint Zeno's patronage of babies is based on a rather strange legend. Apparently, the devil switched Zeno with a goblin at birth. His poor mother suckled her "child" for eighteen years, but he never grew. Fortunately, Zeno was summoned to rescue her, and he made the goblin throw up all the milk into a large vat.

BOYS: SAINT JOHN BOSCO

When Saint John Bosco was eleven years old, he had a dream which indicated he would help and educate poor children. After he had become a priest, he opened a boarding house for neglected boys in Turin, where the youngsters were taught tailoring and shoemaking. John Bosco's work is carried on today by the Salesian Order and the Daughters of Our Lady, Help of Christians, both of which he founded.

CHILDREN: SAINT NICHOLAS OF MYRA

Who could be a more popular choice for the patron saint of children than Saint Nicholas of Myra himself? Legends that grew up around Saint Nicholas reveal that he was a kind, loving person. His patronage of children grew from the story of him bringing three boys back from the dead.

GIRLS: SAINT MARIA GORETTI

Saint Maria Goretti is the patron saint of girls. Because of her unselfishness, piety, cheerfulness, and willingness to work hard, she is considered to be the model on which young girls should pattern their lives. Italy favors her as one of its honored saints.

SCHOOLCHILDREN: SAINT BENEDICT

Saint Benedict, the hermit who founded the great Benedictine Order, is the patron saint of schoolchildren because Benedictine monks have founded many important schools throughout the decades.

STUDENTS: SAINT JEROME

Not many students today spend twenty-two years of their life studying. But when Saint Jerome was asked to write a standard Latin Bible, known as the Vulgate, it took him that many years to complete it. The great scholarship and learning that he applied to his task make him a model for students of all ages.

TEENAGERS: SAINT ALOYSIUS GONZAGA

A rich, young nobleman, Saint Aloysius Gonzaga chose to turn his back on the distractions of the world at age nineteen, and became a member of the Society of Jesus. He contracted the plague in 1591 while nursing others in the hospital and died at age twenty-three. Because of his piety in youth, he was declared the patron saint of teenagers in 1729.

A CLOSING WORD FROM THE AUTHOR

As work on this book was nearing its completion, I visited Montréal to investigate the Cause for Canonization of Blessed Brother André at the beautiful Saint Joseph's Oratory, where Brother André's body is laid to rest. I was inspired to add my name to the list of petitioners supporting his Cause and hope that André may soon be canonized.

After I returned home, I became very ill with an infection that lasted several weeks, delaying work on this book. But throughout the days of high fever and sleeplessness, I always had hope. During the second night of my illness, I dreamed of Brother André. He was a small man in the prime of his life, dressed in black, walking calmly but with a forthright purpose, among those of us who lay awaiting him on our white hospital beds.

He said nothing as he came to my bed; he simply knelt and began to pray. As he did so, his presence seemed to fill the room. I looked up and saw him surrounded by intense white light. He said, "This is the final stage of the healing process which you have worked toward for so many years. It will be a lengthy illness, and afterward you should lead a simple life, eating mainly fruits and vegetables. Of course you may treat yourself," he remarked with a wry smile, "but only occasionally. Live your life so as to inspire others." Then he was gone.

Thank you, Blessed Brother André of Montréal.

CALENDAR OF SAINTS' FEAST DAYS

Watch, dear Lord,
with those who wake, or watch, or weep tonight,
and give your angels charge over those who sleep.
Tend your sick ones, O Lord Christ,
rest your weary ones.
Bless your dying ones.
Soothe your suffering ones.
Pity your afflicted ones.
Shield your joyous ones.
And all for your love's sake. AMEN.

—Saint Augustine
(5th century)

JANUARY

1	St. Peter of Atroa	10	St. Peter Orseolo
2	St. Basil the Great	11	St. Theodosius
3	St. Joseph Mary Tommasi		the Cenobiarch
4	St. Elizabeth Ann Seton	12	St. Marguerite Bourgeoys
5	St. John Nepomucene	13	St. Hilary of Poitiers
	Neumann	14	St. Sava (or Sabas)
6	St. John de Ribera	15	St. Ita
	Blessed André Bessette	16	St. Honoratus of Arles
7	St. Raymund of Peñafort	17	St. Antony the Abbot
8	St. Thorfinn	18	St. Deicolus (or Desle)
9	St. Adrian of Canterbury	19	St. Henry of Finland

JANUARY (CONT.)

20	St. Sebastian	26	St. Paula
21	St. Agnes	27	St. Angela Merici
22	St. Vincent Pallotti	28	St. Thomas Aquinas
23	St. John the Almsgiver	29	St. Gildas the Wise
24	St. Timothy	30	St. Mucian Mary Wiaux
25	The Conversion of St. Paul	31	St. John Bosco

FEBRUARY

1	St. Brigid (or Bride)	17	The Seven Holy Founders of the Servite Order
2	Joan de Lestonnac		
3	St. Blaise		
4	St. John de Britto	18	St. Bernadette
5	St. Agatha	19	St. Boniface of Lausanne
6	St. Paul Miki and companions		
		20	St. Wulfric
	St. Dorothy	21	St. Peter Damian
7	St. Luke the Younger	22	St. Margaret of Cortona
8	St. Jerome Emiliani	23	St. Polycarp
9	St. Apollonia	24	St. Praetextatus
10	St. Scholastica	25	St. Tarasius
11	St. Benedict of Aniane	26	St. Alexander of Alexandria
12	St. Meletius		
13	St. Catherine dei Ricci	27	St. Gabriel of Our Lady of Sorrows
14	St. Valentine		
15	St. Sigfrid of Växjö	28	St. Romanus
16	St. Gilbert of Sempringham		

MARCH

1	St. David	7	St. Drausius
2	St. Chad	8	St. John of God
3	St. Cunegund	9	St. Dominic Savio
4	St. Casimir of Poland	10	St. John Ogilvie
5	St. John Joseph-of-the-Cross	11	St. Oengus
		12	St. Maximilian
6	St. Colette	13	St. Euphrasia

MARCH (CONT.)

14	St. Leobinus	23	St. Turibius
15	St. Longinus	24	St. Gabriel, the
	St. Louise de Marillac		Archangel
16	St. Abraham Kidunaia		(traditional)
17	St. Patrick	25	St. Lucy Filippini
18	St. Cyril	26	St. Braulio
	of Jerusalem	27	St. John of Egypt
19	St. Joseph	28	St. Tutilo
20	St. Cuthbert	29	St. Rupert of Salzburg
21	St. Enda	30	St. Leonard Murialdo
22	St. Nicholas Owen	31	St. Acacius

APRIL

1	St. Hugh of Grenoble	18	St. Galdinus
2	St. Mary of Egypt	19	St. Alphege of
3	St. Richard of Wyche		Canterbury
4	St. Isidore of Seville	20	St. Agnes of
5	St. Vincent Ferrer		Montepulciano
6	St. William of Eskilsoë	21	St. Anselm of
7	St. John Baptist		Canterbury
	de la Salle	22	St. Theodore of Sykeon
8	St. Julia Billiart	23	St. George
9	St. Waldetrudis	24	St. Fidelis Sigmaringen
10	St. Fulbert	25	St. Mark
11	St. Stanislaus of Cracow	26	St. Stephen
12	St. Zeno of Verona	27	St. Zita
13	St. Hermenegild	28	St. Peter Mary Chanel
14	St. Bénezet	29	St. Catherine
15	St. Hunna		of Siena
16	St. Benedict Labre	30	St. Pius V
17	St. Stephen Harding		

MAY

1	St. Richard Pampuri	6	St. Petronax
2	St. Peregrine	7	St. John of Beverley
3	Sts. Philip and James	8	St. Michael
4	St. Florian		(traditional)
5	St. Hilary	9	St. Pachomius

MAY (CONT.)

10	St. Antoninus of Florence	22	St. Rita of Cascia
11	St. Francis di Girolamo	23	St. John Baptist Rossi
12	St. Germanus of Constantinople	24	St. Vincent of Lérins
13	St. John the Silent	25	St. Madeleine Sophie Barat
14	St. Michael Garicoïts	26	St. Philip Neri
15	St. Isidore the Farmer	27	St. Augustine of Canterbury
16	St. John Nepomucene	28	St. Germanus of Paris
17	St. Paschal Baylon	29	Sts. William of Toulouse, Stephen, Raymund, and companions
18	St. Eric of Sweden		
19	St. Dunstan		
20	St. Bernardino	30	St. Joan of Arc
	St. Yves	31	St. Mechtildis of Edelstetten
21	St. Andrew Bobola		

JUNE

1	St. Justin	18	St. Gregory Barbarigo
2	St. Erasmus (or Elmo)	19	St. Juliana Falconieri
3	Sts. Charles Lwanga, Joseph Mkasa, and companions	20	St. Silverius
		21	St. Aloysius Gonzaga
		22	St. Thomas More
4	St. Francis Caracciolo	23	St. Thomas Garnet
5	St. Boniface	24	St. Bartholomew of Farne
6	St. Norbert		
7	St. Antony Gianelli		Birth of St. John the Baptist
8	St. William of York		
9	St. Columba	25	St. William of Vercelli
10	St. Ithamar	26	St. Anthelm
11	St. Barnabas	27	St. Cyril of Alexandria
12	St. Paula Frassinetti	28	St. Irenaeus of Lyons
13	St. Antony of Padua	29	Sts. Peter and Paul
14	St. Methodius I	30	The First Martyrs of the Church of Rome
15	St. Germaine of Pibrac		
16	St. Lutgardis		
17	St. Albert Chmielowski		

JULY

1	St. Oliver Plunket	17	St. Clement of Okhrida
2	St. Otto		and companions
3	St. Thomas	18	St. Bruno of Segni
4	St. Elizabeth of Portugal	19	St. Macrina the Younger
5	St. Athanasius	20	St. Margaret of Antioch
	the Athonite	21	St. Laurence of Brindisi
6	St. Maria Goretti	22	St. Mary Magdalene
7	St. Palladius	23	St. Bridget
8	St. Withburga	24	St. Christina
9	St. Nicholas Pieck		the Astonishing
	and companions	25	St. Christopher
10	Sts. Antony and		St. James the Greater
	Theodosius Pechersky	26	Sts. Joachim and Anne
11	St. Benedict		(parents of Mary)
12	St. Veronica	27	St. Pantaleon
13	St. Cloelia Barbieri	28	St. Samson of Dol
14	St. Camillus de Lellis	29	St. Martha (sister of
	Blessed Kateri		Lazarus)
	Tekakwitha		St. Olaf of Norway
15	St. Bonaventure	30	St. Peter Chrysologus
16	St. Fulrad	31	St. Ignatius of Loyola

AUGUST

1	St. Peter Julian Eymard	12	St. Porcarius
2	St. Eusebius		and companions
3	St. Waltheof	13	St. Maximus the
	(or Walthen)		Confessor
4	St. John Vianney	14	St. Marcellus
5	Sts. Addai and Mari		St. Maximilian
6	St. Hormisdas		Mary Kolbe
7	St. Cajetan	15	The Blessed Virgin Mary
8	St. Dominic		(Her Assumption)
9	St. Oswald of	16	St. Stephen of Hungary
	Northumbria	17	St. Rock (or Roch)
10	St. Laurence	18	St. Helen
11	St. Clare of Assisi	19	St. John Eudes

AUGUST (CONT.)

20	St. Bernard of Clairvaux	27	St. Monica
21	St. Pius X	28	St. Augustine of Hippo
22	St. Sigfrid of Wearmouth	29	St. Medericus (or Merry)
23	St. Rose of Lima		Death of St. John
24	St. Bartholomew		the Baptist
25	St. Louis of France	30	St. Margaret Ward
	St. Patricia	31	St. Aidan
26	St. Elizabeth Bichier des Ages		

SEPTEMBER

1	St. Giles	17	St. Robert Bellarmine
2	St. William of Roskilde	18	St. Joseph of Cupertino
	Blessed André Grasset, St. Sauveur	19	St. Emily de Rodat
		20	St. Eustace
3	St. Gregory the Great	21	St. Matthew
4	St. Rose of Viterbo	22	St. Thomas of Villanova
5	St. Laurence of Giustiniani	23	St. Adamnan of Iona
		24	St. Gerard of Csanad
6	St. Bega (or Bee)	25	St. Albert of Jerusalem
7	St. Clodoald (or Cloud)	26	St. Teresa Couderc
8	St. Corbinian	27	St. Vincent de Paul
9	St. Peter Claver		Sts. Cosmas and Damian
10	St. Nicholas of Tolentino	28	St. Wenceslaus of Bohemia
11	St. Paphnutius	29	Sts. Michael, Gabriel,
12	St. Guy of Anderlecht		and Raphael, the
13	St. John Chrysostom		Archangels
14	St. Notburga		Sts. Rhipsime, Gaiana,
15	St. Catherine of Genoa		and companions
16	Sts. Cyprian and Cornelius	30	St. Jerome

OCTOBER

1	St. Teresa of Lisieux	5	St. Flora of Beaulieu
2	The Guardian Angels	6	St. Bruno
3	St. Thomas Cantelupe		Blessed Marie-Rose
4	St. Francis of Assisi		Durocher

October (cont.)

7	St. Osith	21	St. Ursula and her
8	St. Bridget		maidens
	St. Laurentia	22	St. Philip and
9	St. Dionysius (or Denis)		companions
10	St. Francis Borgia	23	St. John of Capistrano
11	St. Mary Soledad	24	St. Raphael the
12	St. Wilfred		Archangel
13	St. Edward the Confessor		(traditional)
14	St. Callistus I	25	St. Crispin
15	St. Teresa of Avila	26	St. Cedd
16	St. Gerard Majella	27	St. Frumentius
17	St. Ignatius of Antioch	28	Sts. Simon and Jude
18	St. Luke	29	St. Theuderius
19	Sts. Jogues, Brébeuf,		(or Chef)
	and companions	30	St. Alphonsus Rodriguez
20	St. Bertilla Boscardin	31	St. Wolfgang

November

1	All Saints	17	St. Elizabeth
2	St. Marcian		of Hungary
3	St. Martin de Porres	18	St. Odo of Cluny
4	St. Charles Borromeo	19	St. Nerses I
5	St. Bertilla of Chelles	20	St. Edmund the Martyr
	St. Elizabeth	21	St. Albert of Louvain
6	St. Leonard	22	St. Cecilia (or Cecily)
7	St. Willibrord	23	St. Columban
8	St. Godfrey	24	St. Andrew Dung Lac
9	St. Benen (or Benignus)		and companions
10	St. Leo the Great	25	St. Catherine
11	St. Martin of Tours		of Alexandria
12	St. Josaphat Kunsevich	26	St. John Berchmans
13	St. Frances Xavier	27	St. Francis Antony of
	Cabrini		Lucera
14	St. Laurence O'Toole	28	St. Catherine Labouré
15	St. Albert the Great	29	St. Radbod
16	St. Margaret of Scotland	30	St. Andrew

DECEMBER

1	St. Edmund Campion	17	St. Sturmi
2	St. Chromatius	18	St. Flannan
3	St. Francis Xavier	19	St. Anastasius I
4	St. Barbara	20	St. Dominic of Silos
5	St. Sabas	21	St. Thomas
6	St. Nicholas of Bari	22	Sts. Chaeremon,
7	St. Ambrose		Ischyrion, and
8	St. Romaric		companions
	St. Mary, the Blessed	23	St. John of Kanti
	Virgin	24	Sts. Emiliana and Adela
9	St. Peter Fourier	25	St. Anastasia
10	St. Gregory III	26	St. Stephen
11	St. Damasus	27	St. John the Evangelist
12	St. Jane Frances	28	St. Antony of Lérins
	de Chantal	29	St. Thomas à Becket
13	St. Lucy	30	St. Egwin
14	St. John of the Cross	31	St. Silvester I
15	St. Mary di Rosa		
16	St. Adelaide		

PATRON SAINTS OF PROFESSIONS

Accountants	Saint Matthew
Actors	Saint Genesius
Advertising	Saint Bernardine
Anesthesiologists	Saint René
Apothecaries	Saint Raphael
Archaeologists	Saint Helen
Architects	Saint Barbara
Art Dealers	Saint John the Evangelist
Artists	Saint Luke
Astronomers	Saint Dominic
Athletes	Saint Sebastian
Authors	Saint Paul, Saint Francis de Sales
Aviators	Saint Joseph Cupertino, Saint Teresa
Bakers	Saint Nicholas, Saint Meingold
Bankers	Saint Matthew
Barbers	Saints Cosmas and Damian
Beekeepers	Saint Ambrose
Booksellers	Saint John of God, Saint John the Evangelist
Brass Workers	Saint Barbara
Brewers	Saint Nicholas, Saint Wenceslaus
Bridge Builders	Saint Peter
Builders	Saint Vincent Ferrer, Saint Barbara
Cab Drivers	Saint Fiacre
Cabinetmakers	Saint Anne
Carpenters	Saint Joseph
Civil Servants	Saint Thomas More
Clergy	Saint Charles Borromeo
Communications Media	Saint Gabriel
Composers	Saint Cecilia
Confectioners	Saint Joseph
Cooks	Saint Martha, Saint Lawrence

Court Workers	Saint Thomas More
Dairy Workers	Saint Brigid
Dancers	Saint Genesius, Saint Vitus
Dentists	Saint Apollonia
Dietitians	Saint Martha
Doctors	Saint Luke
Domestic Servants	Saint Martha, Saint Zita
Druggists	Saint Raphael the Archangel, Saints Cosmas and Damian
Editors	Saint John Bosco
Engineers	Saint Ferdinand, Saint Joseph
Engravers	Saint John the Evangelist
Farmers	Saint Isidore the Farmer
Firemen	Saint Florian
Fishermen	Saint Andrew, Saint Peter
Florists	Saint Rose of Lima
Gardeners	Saint Dorothy, Saint Sebastian
Goldsmiths	Saint Anastasius, Saint Luke
Grocers	Saint Michael the Archangel
Homebuilders	Our Lady of Loretto
Hospital Workers	Saint Vincent de Paul
Hotel Industry Workers	Saint Amandus
Housekeepers	Saint Martha, Saint Anne
Innkeepers	Saint Julian the Hospitaller, Saint Armand
Jewelers	Saint Eligius
Journalists	Saint Paul, Saint Francis de Sales
Judges	Saint Ives
Laborers	Saint James
Lawyers	Saint Thomas More, Saint Ives

Librarians	Saint Jerome
Locksmiths	Saint Dunstan
Machinists	Saint Hubert
Maids	Saint Zita
Marble Workers	Saint Clement I
Mariners	Saint Michael the Archangel
Masons	Saint Peter
Medical Social Workers	Saint John Regis
Medical Technologists	Saint Albert
Merchants	Saint Armand, Saint Francis of Assisi
Messengers	Saint Gabriel the Archangel
Miners	Saint Piron, Saint Barbara
Musicians	Saint Cecilia
Navigators	Our Lady, Star of the Sea
Needleworkers	Saint Francis of Assisi
Notaries	Saint Luke, Saint Ives
Nuns	Saint Brigid
Nurses	Saint Raphael the Archangel, Saint John of God
Obstetricians	Saint Raymond Nonnatus
Painters	Saint Luke
Policemen	Saint Michael the Archangel
Printers	Saint John the Evangelist
Publishers	Saint Paul, Saint John the Evangelist
Radiologists	Saint Michael the Archangel
Radio Workers	Saint Gabriel the Archangel
Ranchers	Saint Isidore the Farmer
Sailors	Saint Brendan, Saint Michael the Archangel
Salesmen	Saint Lucy
Scientists	Saint Albert
Sculptors	Saint Claude, Saint Luke
Secretaries	Saint Catherine
Servicewomen	Saint Joan of Arc
Shipbuilders	Saint Peter

Shoemakers	Saint Crispin
Silversmiths	Saint Andronicus
Singers	Saint Cecilia, Saint Gregory the Great
Soldiers	Saint Sebastian, Saint George, Saint Joan of Arc
Stained Glass Workers	Saint Mark
Stockbrokers	Saint Matthew
Stoneworkers	Saint Stephen
Surgeons	Saints Cosmas and Damian, Saint Luke
Tailors	Saint Homobonus, Saint John the Baptist
Tanners	Saint Simon Stock, Saint James
Tax Collectors	Saint Matthew
Teachers	Saint Gregory, Saint Francis de Sales, Saint Catherine of Alexandria, Saint John Baptist de la Salle
Telephone Workers	Saint Gabriel the Archangel
Theologians	Saint Augustine, Saint Thomas Aquinas
Tinsmiths	Saint Joseph of Arimathea
Truck Drivers	Saint Christopher
Undertakers	Saint Sebastian
Veterinarians	Saint James
Vocalists	Saint Cecilia
Watchmen	Saint Peter of Alcantara
Weavers	Saint Anastasia, Saint Barnabas
Winemakers	Saint Francis Xavier
Writers	Saint Paul, Saint John the Evangelist

NOTES

1. Kieckhefer and Bond, *Sainthood*, page 3.
2. Walsh, *Butler's Lives of the Saints*, page 335.
3. Gordon, *A Book of Saints*, pages 16-17.
4. *The Book of Common Prayer*, Anglican Church of Canada, page 707.
5. Douillet, *What Is a Saint?*, page 90.
6. Ruffin, *The Life of Brother André*, pages 205-206.
7. Kelly and Melville, *Elizabeth Seton: Selected Writings*, page 19.
8. Maier, *The Catholic World*, page 95.
9. Cunningham, *The Meaning of Saints*, page 29.
10. Desrochers, *Healings Through Good Saint Anne*, pages 167-168.
11. Staniforth, *Early Christian Writings: The Apostolic Fathers*, page 162.
12. Plass, ed., *What Luther Says*, page 1251.
13. Duffy, *The Stripping of the Altars*, page 168.
14. Auclair, *La Vie de Sainte Thérèse d'Avila*, pages 473-474.
15. *One Hundred Saints*, page 199.
16. Oliver, *Songsters and Saints*, page 182.
17. Mullen, *The Latter-Day Saints*, page 41.
18. Ruffin, *Padre Pio: The True Story*, page 241.
19. ———, page 155.
20. Attar, *Muslim Saints and Mystics*, page 13.
21. Ghanananda and Stewart-Wallace, eds., *Women Saints of East and West*, page 169.
22. ———, page 1.
23. ———, page 12.
24. Gordon, *A Book of Saints*, page 20.
25. King, *The Encyclopedia of Mind, Magic and Mysteries*, page 233.

GLOSSARY

Abbey: A monastery led by an abbot or an abbess, having no fewer than twelve monks or nuns.

Acta Sanctorum *(Acts of the Saints)*: Books on the lives of the saints listed according to the dates of their annual feast days.

Anglican: A member of the Church of England. In this context, usually the Anglican Church of Canada.

Annunciation: The announcement to Mary by the archangel Gabriel that she would bear Jesus, celebrated on March 25.

Ascension: The ascent of the body of Jesus into heaven on the fortieth day after the Resurrection (Easter).

Ascetic: A person who leads a meditative life exercising rigorous and severe self-denial.

Assumption: In the Roman Catholic Church, the belief that the body and soul of the Virgin Mary were taken into heaven after her death, celebrated on August 15.

Baptism: In Christianity, the ceremony of admitting a person into the Church by either dipping a person in water or sprinkling him or her with water to symbolize the washing away of sin and spiritual purification.

Beatification: The step before canonization in which the pope declares the deceased to be among the blessed in heaven and that veneration can be expressed locally.

Beatus (Blessed): The title given to one who has been beatified.

Benedictines: Monks and nuns of the order of Saint Benedict, who founded the monastic order in A.D. 529. Also, the "Black Monks."

Bishop: A Christian clergyman of high rank who usually has authority over other clergy and supervises a church district.

Blackrobes: Early Jesuit missionaries to North America. Native Americans called them Blackrobes after the black robes they wore.

Bodhisattva: A person of the Buddhist religion who rejects his state of enlightenment in order to help free humankind from suffering.

Bollandists: Members of the Society of Jesus whose task it is to write an authoritative record on the lives of the saints (the *Acta Sanctorum*).

Buddha: Indian prince, Gautama Siddhartha, whose teachings formed the basis of Buddhism. His followers seek to emulate his example of perfect morality, wisdom, and compassion, resulting in enlightenment.

Buddhism: A religion and philosphy teaching that right thinking and self denial will help the soul to reach Nirvana,a state of divine bliss.

Calendar: A listing or schedule of saints' feast days celebrated by a church, either locally (local calendar) or worldwide (the Roman Catholic calendar).

Canon: The official list of saints as recognized by the Roman Catholic Church.

Canon Law: The body of laws governing a church, in this context, usually the Roman Catholic Church.

Canonization: Declaration by the pope that the beatus is granted the title of "saint" and is to be included in the calendar of saints and venerated worldwide.

Canterbury Tales: An unfinished collection of stories, largely in verse, begun by Geoffrey Chaucer in 1387. The narrators, pilgrims on their way to Saint Thomas à Becket's shrine in Canterbury, tell of life in medieval England.

Carmelites: Monks or nuns of the order of Our Lady of Mount Carmel, founded in Syria around 1160.

Carthusians: A monk or nun of a very strict order founded in 1084 by Saint Bruno at Chartreuse, France.

Catholic: The whole, ancient, undivided Christian Church. In more recent times, it usually, but not necessarily, refers to the Roman Catholic Church, a branch of Christianity headed by the pope in Rome.

Cistercians: Monks or nuns who follow a strict interpretation of the Benedictine rule. Also, the "White Monks."

Confessors: Christians in the early Middle Ages who declared and suffered for their faith, but did not die for it.

Confirmation: In Christianity, a religious ceremony in which a person reaffirms the vows made for him or her at baptism.

Confucianism: Teachings of the Chinese philosopher, Confucius, who emphasized devotion to parents, family and friends, ancestor worship and the maintenance of justice and peace.

Congregation for the Causes of Saints: The section of the Congregation of Rites made up of cardinals that examines all the documentation pertaining to the cause for the making of a saint. It also is charged with the preservation and authentication of relics.

Congregation for the Sacraments and Divine Worship: A group of cardinals that, among other responsibilities, confirms the choice of a patron saint by a group of people.

Consecration: The act of setting something or someone apart as holy or declaring it sacred for religious use.

Crusades: A series of military expeditions during the eleventh, twelfth, and thirteenth centuries in which Christians attempted to take the Holy Land from Islam.

Cultus (cult): The veneration of a saint by public acts, either locally or churchwide, as approved by the pope.

Depositio Episcoporum: One of the original lists of saints which contained the names of deceased bishops.

Depositio Martyrum: The other original list which contained the list of martyrs.

Doctors of the Church: A group of saints who are renowned for their theological writings and their influence on the Church.

Dominicans: Monks or nuns of the order of Saint Dominic, founded in 1215, whose rule of absolute poverty meant that the adherents begged for alms.

Edict of Toleration: An official decree issued jointly by the emperor Constantine and the eastern emperor Licinius in A.D. 313, proclaiming tolerance for all the religions of the Roman Empire. "To the Christians and to all men we decree that there be given free power to follow whatever religion each man chooses so that, whatever gods there be, they may be moved mercifully toward us."

Episcopal Church: A church which is governed by bishops, such as the Anglican church. After the Revolutionary War, Anglican was called Episcopalian in the United States.

Golden Legend: The English translation of the Latin *Legenda Aurea*, written by a thirteenth-century Dominican, James of Voragine, archbishop of Genoa, which contained stories of the lives of the saints.

Hermit: A person who chooses to live alone in a remote place and devotes himself to prayer.

Hinduism: A religion and philosophy of India which developed from several other religions, including Buddhism. Its chief gods are Brahma, Vishnu or Krishna, and Siva.

Holy See: The position, authority, or court of the Roman Catholic pope.

Indult: A special exemption to normal Roman Catholic practice, as granted by the pope.

Invocation of saints: Prayer addressed to the saints asking for blessing, help, inspiration, or support.

Islam: Founded in the seventh century A.D. this religion is based on the laws and teachings contained in the Koran. Its followers, called Muslims, believe that there is one God, named Allah, and that Mohammed is His prophet.

Jesuit: A member of the Society of Jesus, founded by Saint Ignatius Loyola in 1534, as a Roman Catholic order for men.

Judaism: A religion based on the laws and teachings contained in the Old Testament and the Talmud, whose people worship one God, Yahweh or Jehovah; the forerunner of Christianity and Islam.

Koran: The holy book of Islam, written in Arabic by the Prophet Mohammed, as revealed to him by Allah.

Lent: The period of forty days before Easter which commemorates Jesus' fasting in the wilderness. In the Middle Ages, it was the period from Martinmas (Novermber 11) to Christmas, called *Saint Martin's Lent.*

Martyr: Originally meaning "witness," now more commonly refers to someone who chooses to die rather than give up his faith.

Monastery: The buildings or grounds that house a religious order of monks. The equivalent for nuns is a convent.

Monk: A man who retires to a religious community to live under the vows of poverty, obedience, and chastity.

Nun: A woman who devotes herself to religious life in a convent, living under vows of poverty, obedience, and chastity.

Poor Clares: A group of nuns who take strict vows of prayer, poverty, and mortification. It was founded by Saint Clare in 1212 based on the Order of Saint Francis of Assisi.

Pope: The bishop of Rome, supreme head of the Roman Catholic Church, and successor to Saint Peter.

Relic: The bodily remains, belongings, or instruments of the torture and death of a saint.

Roman Martyrology: The official listing of saints as recognized by the Roman Catholic Church.

Rule: The complete set of regulations for a religious order.

Sanctus: The title given to a beatus who has been canonized.

Stations of the Cross: These are a series of fourteen images or pictures, often along the walls of a church, which represent stages of Christ's last journey on His way to the cross. Pilgrims visit each station in succession as a devotional exercise. The stations are:

1. Sentencing by Pilate;
2. the Cross is given;
3. Jesus stumbles;
4. He meets his mother, Mary;
5. Simon is ordered to take the Cross;
6. Saint Veronica wipes his face;
7. He stumbles again;
8. He tells the women of Jerusalem not to weep;
9. He stumbles again;
10. He is disrobed;
11. He is nailed to the Cross;
12. He dies;
13. His body is taken from the Cross;
14. He is entombed.

Stigmata: Formerly a mark burned or cut into the flesh of a criminal or slave. More commonly now, marks resembling the crucifixion wounds of Jesus which appear on some devout persons.

Torah: The scriptures and the law of Judaism contained in the first five books of the Old Testament.

Tribunal: A court of justice or judgment. In Christianity, a group of clergy who determine whether to proceed with a cause for canonization.

Venerable: Someone who is worthy of respect or reverence.

Veneration: The act of showing feelings of deep respect and reverence.

SELECT BIBLIOGRAPHY

Anglican Church of Canada. *The Book of Common Prayer*. Toronto: MacMillan of Canada, 1962.

Attar, Farid al-Din. *Muslim Saints and Mystics*. Translated by A. J. Arberry. New York: Viking Penguin Inc., 1966.

Attwater, Donald. *A Catholic Dictionary*. New York: The MacMillan Company, 1961.

Barthel, Joan. "A Saint for All Reasons," *New York Times Magazine*, September 14, 1975: 13.

Clement, Clara Erskine. *Saints in Art*. Boston: L. C. Page & Company, 1906.

Cunningham, Lawrence S. *The Meaning of Saints*. San Francisco: Harper & Row Publishers, 1980.

Desrochers, Gerard. *Healings Through Good Saint Anne*. Québec: Sainte-Anne-de-Beaupré, 1990.

Dobler, Lavinia. *Customs & Holidays Around the World*. New York: Fleet Publishing Corp., 1962.

Douillet, Canon Jacques. *What is a Saint? A Faith and Fact Book*. Translated by Donald Attwater. London: Burns Oates and Washbourne Ltd., 1958.

Duffy, Eamon. *The Stripping of the Altars: Traditional Religion in England 1400–1580*. London: Yale University Press, 1992.

Dwyer, J. J., ed. *Saints' Names for Boys and Girls*. London: Catholic Truth Society, 1986.

Eastman, Arthur M., ed. *The Norton Anthology of Poetry*. New York: W. W. Norton & Company Inc., 1970.

Foster, Annie H., and Anne Grierson. *High Days & Holidays in Canada*. Toronto: The Ryerson Press, 1961.

Foy, Felician A., and Rose M. Avato. *A Concise Guide to the Catholic Church.* Huntington, Indiana: Our Sunday Visitor, Inc., 1984.

Ghanananda, Swami, and Sir John Stewart-Wallace, eds. *Women Saints of East and West.* London: The Ramakrishna Vedanta Centre, 1972.

Gordon, Anne. *A Book of Saints: True Stories of How They Touch Our Lives.* New York: Bantam Books, 1994.

Hallam, Elizabeth, ed. *Saints: Who They Are and How They Help You.* New York: Simon & Schuster, 1994.

Harrowven, Jean. *Origins of Festivals & Feasts.* London: Kaye & Ward Ltd., 1980.

Hawley, John Stratton. *Saints and Virtues.* Berkeley, California: University of California Press, 1987.

Jacobs, Louis. *Holy Living, Saints and Saintliness in Judaism.* Northvale, New Jersey: Jason Aronson, Inc., 1990.

Karsten, Eileen. *From Real Life to Reel Life: A Filmography of Biographical Films.* Metuchen, New Jersey: The Scarecrow Press, Inc., 1993.

Kelly, Ellin, and Annabelle Melville, eds. *Elizabeth Seton: Selected Writings.* Mahwah, New Jersey: Paulist Press, 1987.

Kieckhefer, Richard, and George D. Bond, eds. *Sainthood: Its Manifestations in World Religions.* Berkeley, California: University of California Press, 1988.

King, Francis X. *The Encyclopedia of Mind, Magic and Mysteries.* Toronto: Smithbooks, 1991.

Krajsur, Richard P., ed. *The American Film Institute Catalog, Feature Films 1961–70.* New York: R.R. Bowker Co., 1976.

Krythe, Maymie R. *All About American Holidays.* New York: Harper & Bros. Publishers, 1962.

Maier, John P. "Miracles and Modern Minds," *The Catholic World,* March/April 1995: 52–58.

McGivern, Father James S. *A Saga of the Church in Canada.* Toronto, Canada: SJ Mission Press.

Morgan, Tom. *Saints: A Visual Almanac of the Virtuous, Pure, Praiseworthy, and Good*. San Francisco: Chronicle Books, 1994.

Moroney, James Patrick. "Saints and Angels: Our Companions on Life's Journey," *The Catholic World*, March/April 1995: 59–63.

Mullen, Robert. *The Latter-Day Saints: The Mormons Yesterday and Today*. Garden City, New York: Doubleday & Co. Inc., 1966.

O'Brien, Felicity. *Saints in the Making*. Dublin, Ireland: Veritas Publications, 1988.

Oliver, Paul. *Songsters and Saints: Vocal Traditions on Race Records*. Cambridge, England: Cambridge University Press, 1984.

One Hundred Saints: Their Lives and Likenesses. New York: Little, Brown and Company, 1994.

Plass, Ewald, ed. *What Luther Says: A Practical In-Home Anthology for the Active Christian*. St. Louis, Missouri: Concordia, 1987.

Ruffin, C. Bernard. *The Life of Brother André: The Miracle Worker of St. Joseph*. Huntington, Indiana: Our Sunday Visitor, Inc., 1988.

Ruffin, C. Bernard. *Padre Pio: The True Story*. Huntington, Indiana: Our Sunday Visitor, Inc., 1991.

Sholapurkar, G. R. Maujpur. *Saints and Sages of India*. Delhi, India: Babbar Printers, 1992.

Somerville, Frank P. L. "Harriet Tubman Honored as a Saint." *Baltimore Sun*, February 20, 1995: 1B.

Tattwananda, Swami. *The Saints of India*. Calcutta, India: R.C. Roy at Printsmith.

Thompson, Sue Ellen, and Barbara W. Carlson, eds. *Holidays, Festivals and Celebrations of the World Dictionary*. Detroit: Omnigraphics, Inc., 1994.

Tierney, Brian, and Sidney Painter. *Western Europe in the Middle Ages, 300–1475*. New York: Alfred A. Knopf, Inc., 1970.

Walsh, Michael, ed. *Butler's Lives of the Saints*. New York: HarperCollins, 1991.

Weingrod, Alex. *The Saint of Beersheba*. Albany, New York: State University of New York Press, 1990.

Weinstein, Donald, and Rudolph M. Bell. *Saints and Society: The Two Worlds of Western Christendom, 1000-1700*. Chicago: The University of Chicago Press, 1982.

Weiser, Francis X. *Handbook of Christian Feasts and Customs*. New York: Deus Books, 1963.

ABOUT THE AUTHOR

CAROLYN TRICKEY-BAPTY is the author of *The Book of Angels: All Your Questions Answered*. After receiving hundreds of letters from *Angels* readers, she took on the challenge of answering questions about saints for her next book.

Carolyn attended Carleton University in Ottawa, where she pursued studies in history and religion. She lives in Hamilton, Ontario, with her husband, Eric, and her son, Jerred.